I may sound as if I'm a few slices short of a loaf, but this is the first time that I feel in control of my life. I got through things by having really, really good friends who helped me and by realising that there is so much out there in the world – the best bits are just there for the taking. We should actively search out happiness, love and adventures. We should travel and squeeze the last drop out of life. We should be out there doing the things that make the stories that you share with your best mate. Just because we are YFAs (Young Female Asians for those who don't know), it doesn't mean that we have a disadvantage or any less of a right to all the good bits of life.

from The Women's Press

Nadya Kassam is a practising Shia Muslim of Kutchi/Gujarati origin. She was born and raised in Tanzania until she was four years old, then her family migrated to Britain. Having completed her degree, she worked in the voluntary sector for six years before starting work on this book. In her spare time she is involved in a Black women's newspaper collective and an Asian women's support group.

Telling It Like It Is

Young Asian Women Talk

Nadya Kassam, editor

LiveWiRE

First published by Livewire Books, The Women's Press Ltd, 1997
A member of the Namara Group
34 Great Sutton Street, London EC1V 0DX

British Library Cataloguing-in-Publication Data
A catalogue record for this book is available from the British Library

ISBN 0 7043 4941 8

Typeset in Bembo 12/14pt by Intype Ltd
Printed and bound in Great Britain by Caledonian International

Acknowledgements

Huge thanks to all the women who participated with such enthusiasm and energy! I'm sorry that we couldn't use every script! I especially admire the courage of those who got their stories to me despite difficult personal circumstances.

Thanks to the teachers and workers who supported women to write; to all my friends, who helped me through challenging times; and to Shaila Shah, for thinking of me as editor. And finally, to The Women's Press for their encouragement and the opportunity to produce this book.

*For my parents, Nabat and Tajdin Ali Kassam,
and my brother Karim*

Contents

Introduction

When The Women's Press approached me to edit this book I was thrilled; editing a book was on my 'list of things to do' in my life. I was nervous of the responsibility, and yet felt ready for the challenge. It was an important project to be involved in – the first time that young Asian women were to be given a space to speak for themselves.

As Asian women, we often feel isolated and alone because our communities do not usually allow us to speak freely. We have many identities which we juggle every day, making choices and decisions which reflect us as individuals. The media always appears to focus on the tragic consequences of being an Asian woman in the West; mental health problems, suicide and forced marriages do exist, as they do in many other communities, but they are only a small part of our experience.

There is little written evidence to show how powerful, funny and eloquent young Asian woman are. I realised this as soon as I began receiving scripts from women. The quality of all the pieces was extremely high, expressing concerns, problems and solutions – whether they were angry, witty or sad. I feel that this book is an accurate picture of young Asian women's lives.

Accounts range from women rebelling against tradition in order to fit in with their peers, to passionately defending their culture and religion. Themes range from education and boyfriends to disability and religion. A few contributions are extremely controversial – for example, being abused by a family friend or coming out as a lesbian, but all are positive accounts of the way these young women are succeeding in combining who they are with what they want. I have chosen scripts that reflect a wide range of voices from different classes, religions, (dis)ability and sexuality, mixed heritages and cultures – young Asian women 'telling it like it is' for themselves.

I felt very strongly that a book of this nature should exist; it's something I didn't have in my own teenage years. It was funny to realise that the same devices and subterfuges that I employed to be with my friends are still widespread among Asian teenagers today! I hope this book serves as a mirror for young Asian women and provides evidence that they are not alone; many others have the same dilemmas every day.

Scripts came from women in cities, towns and even from villages across the country. Schools, refuges, writing projects, youth groups and community centres all contributed. The range of support and hindrance to the work has been enormous; many parents were surprisingly co-operative, even going to the lengths of faxing a script to a daughter on holiday in order to get her amendments! However, I also found that some Asian head teachers felt it 'inappropriate' to 'single out' Asian girls for such an opportunity.

Parents and teachers may learn something from *Telling It Like It Is*. Young Asian women *can* be trusted, we *do* love and respect our families and traditions, but we also need to be ourselves and find our own identities. If this book helps just one young Asian woman to feel that she is not alone, it will have been worth the months of hard work.

I also hope it will encourage Asian women to continue writing their stories and documenting their experiences for others and themselves, as there are still many more stories to be told. Above all, I hope that readers find *Telling It Like It Is* enjoyable, fascinating and fun to read.

Clubbing

The gig was the talk of the year. For me, this was to be my first-ever night club. It was a 'daytime' do, for young Asians who were not allowed out at night. Everyone I knew was going. Exams had just finished and everyone had just one thing on their minds – having a good time. I was determined to go.

I had told my brother about it, and thankfully, he wasn't the typical Asian brother type, who went ballistic when you mentioned that the opposite sex were going to be in the vicinity. He was quite sweet about it and gave me the 'I know what blokes are like' routine, but I appreciated his concern. It was actually my sister who had a go at me and said why couldn't I wait until I was eighteen!

The night before the gig, I tried on my dress for the fourth time. It was long, and emphasised my figure.

Nothing too tarty – my parents had brought me up well! Lastly, and most importantly, I phoned my friends to confirm what we were going to say. We had to make sure that our stories matched. Only a few could tell their parents the truth and didn't need to lie.

The next morning, I woke up early. Boy, was I excited! I bathed and brushed my teeth just a bit longer and went down to eat my breakfast. Trying to act normally, I held back the temptation to eat it all in three bites.

'Who is going today, behta?' my mother asked.

'Oh, just all of us, it should be a laugh,' I replied.

'When will you be back home?'

'About seven o'clock.'

'Seven o'clock?' she asked. 'What will you be doing at the cinema until seven o'clock? Please be home by six.'

I tried to argue for more time but it was no good.

Walking up the stairs to my bedroom, I imagined what it would be like. Would I meet the man of my dreams? What if a relative saw me and reported me to my mum and dad? What if they found out another way? What if there was a disaster? I realised I was being very paranoid and stopped thinking 'what if'.

I put my dress on for the fifth and final time, styled my hair and applied foundation. I looked in the mirror for the last time and smiled cheekily to myself. Two devilish horns seemed to grow out of my head. I'll never go to heaven, I thought, but frankly, at that point, I didn't care. I wanted to have a good time with my friends, not reserve a place in heaven.

I called out 'bye' to my mum as I headed out of the front door and made my way to Nita's house to do the rest of my make-up and meet the others.

As we got off the train, a group of boys in their late teens herded off as well and walked up to the club ahead of us, singing an old Indian bhangra song, badly. They acted like they were going to a football match, not a club. Great, a bunch of yobbos, I thought, that's all we need. If this was a taste of things to come, I didn't want to go.

In the queue to get in, everyone looked the same to me. A bit like they had been made on a factory line. All the girls seemed to have bright red lipstick on and golden-orange streaks in their hair, held in place by half a can of hairspray. All the guys had baggy jeans on with either a checked shirt or sweatshirt and trainers. It was taking forever to get in because the bouncers were searching everyone. As we waited our turn, two men got out of a car and my heart skipped a beat when I saw them with cameras and microphones. Of all the times for them to show up! I could just picture it; my family settling down to relax in front of the TV and behold, there I would be, desperately trying to hide my face. Of all the people there, I knew it had to happen to me and I'm sure my parents believed in the death penalty as punishment, even if the rest of the country didn't!

The crew set up their equipment by the entrance and I hid as well as I could, until I got in. Putting our

6

bags in the cloakroom, we explored the inside of the building. There was a main dance floor and a stage, with a side section for the DJs. There were sofas around the edge of the dance floor and three bars, which were all overlooked by a gallery upstairs.

We all got seats near the dance floor. The music was bhangra, which wasn't really our type of music and I didn't feel comfortable dancing to it. We waited for it to change to swing or jungle. We waited all night. Hours passed and it was *still* bhangra. I didn't want to admit it, but I was bored. I think I would have had a better time at my grandma's feeding her cat! Finally, the music changed. It was as if God had sent down a little ray of sunshine. We all ran on to the dance floor before the music changed again.

I began to relax a bit and we all started to enjoy ourselves, despite the film crew still lurking around the club. Then Nita, who has more hormones than the rest of us put together, started to look for boys. She was acting like a wild animal hunting! It was thanks to her that I met him.

It happened as one guy walked past Nita, and, in her usual way, she managed to start dancing with him. Then, his friend just happened to walk past. He smiled at me and I smiled back. He moved closer and we danced together. From then on, there was nothing but electricity . . . I felt like Gazza scoring a goal! It was brilliant!

Eventually, the gig came to an end. The men with the cameras had left and we both knew we had to go.

We said our goodbyes, swearing to see each other again and hopefully we will. I just hope that my parents and the rest of the nation don't see him (on TV) before I do!

Ishman Tardho

My First Date

I am sixteen years old and I live in a village in Suffolk. My family is the only Asian family in the area and all my friends are white. My parents are Muslim and were born and brought up in India. They came over to England in 1958, long ago enough, I thought, to become accepted, but we are still so different from all the other families around us. Our colour, traditions and beliefs stick out a mile. A lot of my friends do not understand what being an Indian Muslim means, only that I can't go to discos, go out with boys or drink. I have to admit that I am jealous of my friends who aren't bothered by the idea of 'sin' – they are free to enjoy their teenage years. I'm even jealous of my friends' parents – they have a relationship, mine have an arrangement. So sometimes, even I can only see my background as a restriction.

Last summer, just after my fifteenth birthday, I started going roller-skating. I passed it off as a sport to my mum and dad, even though the rink is more like a club. My friends could all skate and I couldn't. I often ended up looking like a prat, flat on my face, even though I used to make an effort with my appearance, like wearing nice clothes and make-up, because it was my only opportunity to meet boys.

One Sunday I met a boy called Kevin. He was seventeen and was training to be a mechanic. I actually fancied one of his mates, but after we all got chatting I found out that the one I liked was already going out with someone. Kevin, on the other hand, was available. I can't say that I fancied him exactly, but he seemed to fancy me and at the end of the night he asked me out for a drink. I said yes but explained that he would not be able to ring me to arrange it – I would have to ring him because my parents were strict and would hit the roof if they found out I was going out with a boy.

I didn't tell anyone else, apart from my best friend who I really trusted, that I was going to go out with him. I had never been out with a boy before. I never really talked about boys anyway, because actually meeting someone I liked and who liked me, and hiding it from my parents, seemed impossible. But Kevin seemed to accept things were going to be difficult.

The following week, I rang him from a phone box and arranged to meet him. It was during the school holidays so I couldn't make up a story about having to do something for school. I told my mum I was going for a walk and that I would be back before it was dark.

She didn't say anything, although I was wearing make-up and my most trendy clothes. I had been fantasising about this moment for so long. My first date! My first boyfriend! A light went on in my head – I could be normal like the other girls and it was worth the risk. I was excited, but not about meeting him; I was excited because I felt like I was living at last!

I met him by my school. He had a car and we drove to a pub just outside the village. I had an orange juice and he had a beer. I was very quiet, perhaps because I was nervous and worried about my parents. He did make an effort but I couldn't relax. I came across as very cool, so he started telling me that I was weird. That just made things worse. I did try to be more chatty. I asked him about his parents and he told me he was half-Iranian. His dad was a Muslim but wasn't strict at all. I couldn't believe it! Someone else who was a Muslim in Suffolk! But Kevin couldn't under-stand why I was so interested in that part of him. I was disappointed that the only near-Muslim boy in the whole of Suffolk could not understand how much I needed understanding! Every time he said I was weird, I felt further and further away from him.

So we had nothing in common. He couldn't under-stand why I was so anxious and I think he thought that I was making it all up because I didn't really want to go out with him.

At nine o'clock, I made him take me home. It was already dark, but I still made him drop me off a few doors away from my house. As I was getting out of the car, he asked whether he could see me again. I asked him whether he liked me and he said he did.

11

Then he kissed me. I had never been kissed before. I didn't feel anything.

He drove off and I went indoors to face my mum who shouted at me for walking around in the dark. I phoned Kevin the next day and told him I didn't want to see him again. He said he didn't mind about my parents but I insisted that it would be too difficult. He was angry but he couldn't say anything to change my mind.

I felt glad that I had been out with a boy and that we had kissed, but I was disappointed that I hadn't felt anything. I didn't even tell my friends about it. I still didn't feel like one of them. Looking back on it now, I think I decided to finish it because I didn't really like him and I used my parents as an excuse. I think if I had felt something for him, I would have tried to carry on seeing him even though it would have been difficult. I was and am still different; feeling accepted is more than being asked out on a date.

Mina

We Are All Human

My name is Halema Begum. I am a sixteen-year-old Bengali girl and have just finished my GCSEs. I am a Sunni Muslim, who was born in Yorkshire and brought up in London.

First of all, I would like to talk about my family. My parents come from a part of Bangladesh called Sylet and I have visited there twice. I have a very large family of three brothers and four sisters. I also have lots of nieces and nephews.

The good thing about my family is that we live together and support each other, and we are also close to our relatives. There are disadvantages of a large family as well. Obviously, there isn't any quiet time at home and I have two sisters who I fight with continuously! But I must say that I can't imagine living without them.

I am always expected to dress sensibly. My family does not mind me wearing anything, as long as it falls within the definition of Islamic dress, and does not show off my body. So, at home I wear shalwar kameez and when I go out with my friends, I wear trousers, shirts, long skirts and dresses. Me and my friends like to wear fashionable clothes, but I do not follow blindly, I do have the sense to realise when fashions are not Islamically acceptable. I think that society puts pressure on Asian girls to wear Western clothes. This is all right, but we should not neglect our Asian clothes as they are our tradition and we should not lose our cultural roots.

I am not allowed to date anybody. This is not a problem now, but it used to be. When my friends went out with boys, I would feel left out. In fact, most of my friends are not allowed to date either, but they would go out without their parents knowing. I have decided now that I would prefer not to have a boy-friend, because I don't need the hassle, the heartache and, most of all, I don't want to lose my parents' trust. I think that all I need now is a good education.

My family follows the cultural way of finding a partner, which is usually described as an 'arranged marriage'. This does not mean forcing a young girl into an unsuitable match, as the popular image portrays. In my family, parents find a suitable partner, the couple are allowed to see each other if they want, and then the couple have the final say in the matter. This is why I do agree with this system, but I also know that some girls are still being forced into it, which is totally wrong. I think the success or failure of a marriage depends on the couple. They make the marriage work or fail. So, I think that everyone should have the right to say 'no' if they are really unhappy with their family's choice of partner. After all, you are the ones who are supposed to live together!

My hobby at home, believe it or not, is gardening! I love flowers. During my spare time, I help my mum in the garden, but my friends don't know about this. They will probably think I have gone mad! Some people think gardening is boring but I enjoy it because it is rewarding. I am really proud of myself when I see the plant that I grew from a tiny seed.

My other hobbies are reading, painting, watching TV and looking after my cat, Shadow. At school, my favourite subjects are history and art, and I also like PE.

My ambition is to go back to Bangladesh and see some of the world. That would be brilliant, because I want to know what the world has to offer. Before that, I think I need to get a good education and a good job.

At school, I used to be called a 'paki'. I know lots of other people who have had to put up with racism. When I was younger, I used to ignore it, but that made it worse. So, when I got to around fourteen, I thought to myself that I don't have to put up with this anymore. Then I started to stick up for myself and say 'Yes, paki and proud of it!' That's when the name calling stopped. People who call Asians 'paki' don't know the meaning of the word. Actually, in Indian languages, it means 'pure', and it is short for Pakistan, so there's nothing offensive about it.

I don't think that all white people are racists. I have lots of friends who are white and they happen to respect me and my Asian friends. I think people should not judge others by the way they look or where they come from. It's your personal qualities that should be judged. At the end of the day, we are all human even though we have differences.

Halema Begum Aktar

A Letter to My Brother

Dear Jasmit

Thank you so much for pointing out what is so desperately wrong with my life, according to *your* narrow-minded views.

I can see that in your eyes, I am an emotionally unstable teenage Asian female, who knows nothing about her identity or culture. Do you know how many times I used to question my identity? It was a bit hard not to, when you were constantly pointing out that the colour of my skin was more 'white' than 'brown' and that I 'acted white'. According to you, I was 'sad' because I didn't listen to bhangra music.

Well, let me tell you, just because I don't listen to bhangra, it doesn't mean that I am trying to adopt

17

another culture. I'm not a sheep that follows what everyone else does, I'm an individual who has the right to make my *own* decisions.

For your information, I am not uncultured; our parents did a damn good job of bringing me up. I know what is morally wrong and right, I have morals, principles and opinions. I know how to speak my mother tongue and I wear my national dress. Just because I don't parade up and down the High Street on Diwali with a khanda in my hand, bragging about my religion (and making a total fool of myself in the process), that does not mean I am denying my culture or religion. Just because *you* find it acceptable to openly display those religious and cultural signs, it doesn't make you automatically better than me!

You're always saying that I'll be lucky to get married and have children, the way I am. Is that what you think? That I will spend my life just as somebody's wife, with no identity of my own, content to look after the house and stay in the kitchen all day? Do you *really* think that all Asian wives need to keep them happy is a new microwave?

The answer is NO! I don't know which century you are living in, but I'm telling you one thing for sure – being an Asian woman is not a punishment or a restriction. The world is my oyster and my life will be what I make it!

I don't know where you got this attitude from. You think that women are the possessions of men and can only have a future through their husbands. I suppose

18

you got this from hanging around with your cronies who were all brought up as typical Asian boys? They are all given everything their hearts desire by their parents, and yet, when they come home drunk or high on drugs, their parents wonder where they went wrong! So, this is my message for the parents who give everything to the boys: GET OUT OF THE STONE AGE! It may have made sense in your generation, but things are different now. Stop undermining your daughters, they are not going to believe in themselves when equality isn't even practised at home!

I really feel like screaming when I think of all the times you've made me feel low. You've always undermined me, made me feel stupid, even when I got higher grades than you. You kept saying that it didn't matter what I got, I wasn't going to get anywhere anyway. You were planning to become a doctor or an engineer, all I was going to do was become a wife or mother!

Well, I'm writing to thank you! Because of all your narrow-minded ideas and scorn, I have become stronger and more independent. You fool, without even realising it, you were preparing me for real life. I am more determined than ever to get an education. I intend to get a decent job and spend my life comfortably, not dependent on any man. I want to be as free as possible and I want to be *me*, not an extension of someone else. I don't want to live my life in someone's else's shadow.

I finally have enough confidence to speak out and

say 'Yes, I'm a young Asian woman and I'm going to do something with my life!'

Your loving sister,

Raj

Raj Kelair

Facing up to Bullying

Hi, my name is Valene Marie Coutinho. I consider myself to be Indian first, as my father is Goan and my mother is half-Madrasi and half-Italian – so I am a mixture.

Being bullied has to be my most vivid memory. As I am a devout Catholic, my parents sent my brother and me to a Catholic school run by Irish nuns. I was put into the first year as an eight-year-old and would stay at that school until I was eleven.

For the whole of the first year, I always went home crying. Even now, it still hurts because all I wanted was to have real friends of my own.

My first day at school was terrible. I had never experienced racial discrimination in my infant school, so it was a shock to me when people judged me by my colour, instead of my personality. There was one

21

girl called Karen, who made me cry on my first day. She was Spanish. I can't remember exactly what happened, but I do remember her shouting names at me in the playground because I was brown-skinned, which really upset me. From then on, I was often ignored and when allowed to speak, I was looked at as if I was garbage.

The bullying was mainly done by the girls in my own class. They were all white, except one who was Indian, but she was very snobbish and did not think I was worthy of her friendship or her time. Most of the boys never noticed me or kept their distance, but there was one boy who was nice to me and would make me laugh if he saw that I was upset. He became one of my best friends and I would always sit next to him in class.

I felt embarrassed and stupid every time the girls ignored me, or looked at me as if I was worthless. I have many memories of just sitting in a corner of the playground, bored and, more than anything else, lonely. As time went on, I learned to cope with the snide comments, the occasional slap on the face and racist remarks, by keeping it to myself. Somehow I managed to make 'friends' or so I thought. But these so-called friends always managed to make me the butt of their jokes and would boss me around. I can remember one time, in the third year, when I was reading alone at lunchtime. Suddenly, a group of girls from my class came and circled around me, snatched my book away and slapped me hard on my face. It was such a shock that I just stood there holding my face and cried bitterly. This seemed to have no effect on them, apart from amusing them. They all just stood there laughing and they threw my book in the bin. I never reported the girls or told anyone, because I felt so ashamed. I was ashamed because they made me cry and I didn't even have a chance to retaliate. Later on, they came up to me and said it was just a joke, that I shouldn't be such a baby over it. This made me even more ashamed of myself, because I believed them. They had once again managed to make a fool of me and make me think it was all my fault at the same time. For that, I never forgave them.

There was only one teacher who was okay. He was my second-year teacher and he'd always listen to me and believed everything I had to say. He used to stick up for me against the whole class. Once we all had a maths test. On that day, I had a terrible headache and he sent me to sickbay. He agreed to let me do the test at home. The next day, I returned the test to him and scored quite highly. Most of the others started complaining that I had cheated. I was mortified, almost in tears. For me, that had been a big achievement, as I was not particularly strong in maths. However, my teacher immediately stood up for me, shouting at anyone who called me a cheater. I was at my happiest in his class.

I only ever told my mum what was happening and she would console me. I never, however, let her tell the teachers because I was ashamed. I thought that it was meant to happen to me, so I left it. It never really got better or easier the whole time at that school.

Because I accepted it as a fact of life, I didn't fight it.

It was strange, but during my four years at this school, I never looked on my being treated badly as bullying. To me, it was a way of life, something that happened to everyone. I realise now that I had no real friends, that my years there were unhappy and that I looked upon myself as someone below them, who wasn't worthy of their friendship.

It wasn't until I had watched a children's TV programme that I realised I was being bullied and that it wasn't meant to just happen to everyone. I had always thought that bullying was always violent, with the victims being beaten up or having their money or books stolen. Suddenly, as I watched, the presenter was telling the viewers that name-calling and general bitchiness was a form of bullying and I realised that it was happening to me.

But for the life of me, I couldn't understand why it had happened. What was so wrong with me? Why me? The answers were difficult to find. Perhaps they were jealous of me, my mum said. I couldn't comprehend why they would be. They were pretty, smart, popular and had many friends – everything I dreamed of having. My mother said they were jealous of me because all their parents liked me. Their parents thought I was a little angel. All of them loved my long, thick dark hair and big brown eyes. For this, the girls hated me; they wanted their mothers to adore them, not me. So they made my life miserable.

By the time I came to my present school, my self-esteem was at an all-time low. However, I did manage to make friends – real friends who liked and respected me for who I was, not judging me by the colour of my skin. These friends showed me that I was worth listening to and worth knowing. Being different was what made me special. Difference is what makes everybody unique. This was when I slowly began to come to terms with what had happened to me.

My friends now are mixed, but mainly Indian. I have three Muslim friends, one Iraqi, one Pakistani and one half-French, half-Bengali. I have two Indian-Japanese friends and the others are white or African Caribbean. My confidence has picked up, as well as my studies and I have become a much happier person, but I will never forget my years at primary school.

For anyone out there who is being made unhappy like I was, stand up for yourself, always. Don't ever think you are below them, because then they have won. If they don't appreciate you as you are, they don't deserve you and your company. Respect and love yourself first, before trying to fit in with the crowd. If people like you for who you are, they are genuine friends. Always remember, a bully is a coward, someone who thinks you won't stand up to them. Prove them wrong and make them afraid of you. Hit them if they hit you, call them names if they call you names and never ever fear them – they're not worth it.

As I am a much stronger person and I believe in myself, I know I would now stand up for myself each and every time anyone picked on me. If I had to go through it all again, that's what I would do differently.

But I don't dwell on the past because then I would be tormenting myself even more. Never look back, always look forward. Think of all the things you want in life and go for them, no matter what.

Valene Coutinho

Falling for the
Wrong Boy

Out of all my friends, I had always been the cool-
headed one, trying to study hard and not really caring
to notice the opposite sex. All around me, my friends
were swapping boyfriends or sleeping around, while I
was more content to read a book. I had never had any
romantic feelings for a bloke, or had the urge to go
out with any of them. I had a personality defect when
it came to getting close to someone.

I don't really know where I got this attitude from.
At home, my parents had given me the standard, very
brief talk about boys (ie don't do anything with them!).
My father could lecture me for hours and hours about
drinking, smoking, drugs and so on, but never directly
about boys. I suppose this is because my parents never
suspected that I was capable of doing anything with
the opposite sex!

Anyway, I suppose I had enforced all of this on myself so much that I began to wonder if I was abnormal – maybe I had some hormones missing? I had never had a crush on a boy, let alone really liked one. But then, one day, I began to fall for *him*.

I started to spend more and more time with him and even though we were so different, we seemed to 'click'. However, he wasn't exactly the type of person I could take home to meet Mummy and Daddy. He was fairly clever, but he was arrogant, usually high on drugs and – Black!

At first, I just ignored my feelings, because I couldn't admit them to myself and also because I didn't know if he felt the same way. I suppose part of the problem was that I was still a 'good' Hindu girl when it came to boys, and I considered myself to be fairly intelligent, compared to his usual 'airhead' type girl-friends. However, when he started making sexual comments as I walked past, when our eyes would have no trouble meeting across a crowded room and when he looked like he was undressing me with his eyes, we knew that our friendship would never be platonic again.

Being different races didn't stop us from having a relationship. When we were alone together for the first time, it finally struck me – I was an Indian, and even after all that was enforced on me by family and friends, I still found myself falling for a Black boy. I used to think about how his cocoa brown skin looked next to my creamy brown skin when we held hands; how his hair was so black and curly, compared to my very straight black hair. I think that I was very visually aware of the race factor.

Anyway, he was probably the worst bloke I could have fallen for, because he really had a way with words, the gift of the gab, definitely! With a few sweet words about how gorgeous I was, I melted in his arms and ended up having my first kiss. I finally discovered my hormones! It was just like a romantic novel. I know that most people say that first kisses can be disasters, but mine was brilliant. At seventeen I was finally going through my first bumpy romance ride.

I even started acting like a school kid – and that's when it all began. In my college, Black–Indian relationships just didn't happen and were not accepted. But hiding from people in order to spend even a few moments with him, put more excitement into my life. Rumours began to spread like wildfire, but neither of us cared. I started to dump my friends and get into drugs a bit, which maybe clouded my judgement.

Even though it's over now, I can truthfully say that one of the reasons I went along with it was because it was 'taboo' and seen as 'wrong'. That's one of the things that made it so exciting – knowing that what I was doing was not really accepted or tolerated, and not knowing what I would do if (God forbid) my parents ever found out. I'm glad that things stopped, because I was starting to live life really dangerously, taking lots of risks. Still, I don't regret anything that happened and I'm getting on with my life. Our breaking up didn't have anything to do with being from different races and cultures, although that did sometimes complicate things.

When I was with him, I looked beyond the colour of his skin. I wasn't trying to prove anything by being with him, I liked him for what he was inside. Once I had stripped away the colour of his skin and his image, I had found a really wonderful person.

Jill Akera

Making My Own Culture

Do you know the feeling when you know exactly what you want to say, but instead, you bite your tongue? Or, you know exactly what you want to do – but you feel you can't do it? Sadly, I do. I also know that these feelings make you act differently with different groups of people. For instance, I generally act outgoing, loud and open with my friends and hide from them the extent to which I am actually restricted by my parents. I hide the way most Bengali girls are supposed to act at home, because it may be hard for people outside our culture to understand. Bengali girls take on a quieter, more obedient role at home, especially around our fathers and elder members of the community. Some girls are expected to act the same way around their elder brothers, who can be more restrictive than parents. Knowing this, I don't personally feel the loss of not having an older brother, even though I was made to feel that way when I was growing up! You conform to their expectations, however much you don't want to, and by putting up this act, you somehow lose yourself in a split personality.

The above is probably the same for many women, whatever their backgrounds, but I cannot help thinking that I would not want the many things I want, hate the many things I hate, if I had not been born and brought up in Britain. I imagine that if I had been brought up entirely in Bangladesh, I would not hate the male-dominated society I live in and the restrictions I am under, just because I am a woman and because of fear of gossip in the community. My parents do not mind me being friends with boys at university, or talking to them in the street. But, because of what others in the community might think, I am not allowed to give them my telephone number or invite them to my house.

This is not to say that I see living in Britain as a loss; on the contrary, I see it as an unimaginable benefit. Unlike many of my Asian friends, I tend to forget the racism and barriers I have encountered growing up here, and realise how open-minded and strong it has made me. I speak out for what I believe in, without feeling inferior because I am a woman; I am more tolerant of other people and their way of life, however much it differs from mine. The hard part about living in Britain for me – as I am sure it is for many Asian women – is that I feel torn between two cultures. While on one hand, I want to be loyal and maintain the culture my parents have brought me up in, with its sense of family security, the respect it gives to its elders and the air of magic that it spins during social gatherings, I also want to embrace the good parts of the one I see around me in Britain. This includes the respect that British culture gives to women, allowing them to be more independent. I take for granted being allowed to walk around in public, unchaperoned, which would be unheard-of in Bangladesh. There, I would have to be aided by a respectable male. I am also envious of women who reach the age of twenty-five without feeling the threat of marriage lurking around them.

To incorporate British culture into the Bengali community is easier said than done, not only because of the pressures of conforming that the elder members of my community put upon Bengali girls, (we must willingly accept roles of being passive, subordinate and dutiful all for the sake of family pride), but also because of the pressures from the other Asian girls I grew up with. Many of them do take on the roles of wife and mother – which I have no argument against – but it does make it harder for me to be different. The common reaction from such girls, on hearing my views that men should take equal responsibility with housework and women should not have to be tied down to children, is how Westernised I am. Therefore, at an early age, even when I knew I strongly opposed these beliefs, I felt I had to agree so they didn't see me as being deviant or judgemental, and most importantly, accepted me as one of them. This made me behave differently from how I felt; I used to pretend that I could cook and act as if I accepted the view that women are dependent on men. I feel ashamed to tell you my reaction when a friend told me that she saw a man beating a woman as his right, just as that of a mother hitting a child who has misbehaved. I knew what she was saying was wrong – but I am sad to say I didn't argue against her, and my silence was as bad as agreeing with her.

Just as these girls made it hard for me to show my true feelings about our culture, so did Bengali girls who ridiculed and rejected it as being totally negative. I felt that I had to defend our culture against these girls at all costs. Some would label traditional girls as being 'typical' and 'weak'. With these girls, I would pretend that everything in our culture was wonderful. I know their narrow view of our culture is wrong, as many girls like me are continuing their education and establishing careers before and after marriage, although many do accept arranged marriages, knowing of the restrictions of our culture upon women, and the strong emphasis on family loyalty. I cannot decide which woman is stronger; the one who makes the 'little' sacrifice of her own happiness for the sake of her parents, or the one who rejects the notions of an arranged marriage and sacrifices a quiet life for her own happiness.

So far I have talked about the difficulty of growing up with peers who have either totally accepted or totally rejected our ways, however I realise that there are now more women like me, who accept some of the traditional ways, but still feel restricted. It was only when I learned to open up to such women about my feelings that I found I could open up to close non-

Bengali friends, without feeling a sense of disloyalty to my community. The truth is that I feel closer to girls from my own culture, because I feel defensive about our cultural differences with non-Bengali friends, whether they are white, Black or other types of Asian. I do feel left out sometimes, when they are allowed to do things that I am not, such as staying out late. Despite having a closer connection with Bengali girls, I know we are still not totally open with each other, because we don't want the other person to be judgemental about our parents or our behaviour. This does often leave me feeling guilty of deceiving my friends and my parents. The only people I feel I can confide in are my sisters and brothers, as we are in the same position, and I'm not worried about being judged by them.

Sometimes I do not understand why I accept all that I am supposed to, when actually, I don't agree with a lot of it. It is hard for me to explain my discontent to my parents, not only because they have given me more opportunities than many of my friends have had, but also because I've had more opportunities than my parents themselves and I don't want to seem ungrateful. At these times of confusion and frustration, even the two languages I speak become a barrier. I feel I cannot explain properly in Bengali the thoughts I have in English, so I do not speak at all. For example, on the matter of choice, I find it hard to explain that it is not necessarily the actual decision I make that is important, but the *ability to make a choice* that matters. In Bengali, I would have to suggest my choice to my parents first.

I also feel like a hypocrite when I tell my friends to accept the ways of our culture, such as consenting to marriage when they do not feel ready, (but they do it as they do not want to hurt or disappoint their parents), when actually, I would like to tell them to speak out about their true feelings. These situations make me realise how involved in my culture I really am; I *do* allow gossip to affect me, and I end up warning my little sister not to be seen with her friends and their boyfriends. I also tell my brothers and sisters to lower their voices when we have unknown visitors in the house.

The extent we each feel trapped and want to change our culture differs. This is why, even amongst good friends, I fear the other person will not understand, so I hide my feelings and act in ways which I feel are expected and acceptable. Ultimately, I act like a stranger amongst my own people.

Shaheena Begum Mossabir

Alternative Christmas

I can't imagine living out of Britain, especially if the alternative was Asia or Africa. I was born here, in London and have grown up in this country, surrounded by all religions and cultures, whereas my dad, brothers and sister were born in Tanzania, and my mum in Kenya. I was born after my parents moved to England over sixteen years ago. England may be a Christian country but in my eyes, it is mixed with every religion I know.

I wouldn't call myself religious, but I do believe in God. Being Hindu, we have many festivals throughout the year, including Diwali, the festival of light, and others which my family don't celebrate. At Christmas time in Britain we are locked in a fantasy world with Christmas trees, snow, crackers and turkey. The world seems a better place at Christmas time, and all your problems disappear for a few days until the New Year. I'm not putting down Christmas, but all we get to do in my family is listen to the Queen's speech and watch films that are either repeats or boring.

Everyone has time off work or school to celebrate Christmas, but for Diwali, which is our New Year, we have to book our leave in advance and sometimes, when this gets difficult, you don't enjoy yourself as much. In India, people have time off for Diwali and can celebrate it properly. They get holiday time for it, just like for Christmas holidays in Britain. My family doesn't have the chance to get together with the whole family and celebrate as much as we would like to; some of our relatives live quite far away and some still have to work. There are other things for us to do, like going to dances and having talent shows, but it's not the same.

Diwali is enjoyable here, but in India, people can dance in the street because the climate is better. In London this can happen in certain areas, but you have to get up really early in order to miss the traffic! Diwali is a time to dress up, get together with your family, make special foods and generally party, but you still have to worry about waking up early the next day so you can go to work or school. For Christmas, you can party all night and the holiday is arranged for you, so you don't have to worry.

I have only celebrated Diwali in Britain, so I'm not sure just how different it would be in Tanzania, for example, but I would like to see what it's like.

As for other aspects of being Asian, my parents aren't very strict about who I marry. Well, I hope not! I'll probably only really find out when the time comes. It seems to be more strict in India and women get married at an earlier age there. Women here tend to concentrate on their education and careers first, before planning marriage and kids, and that's what I plan to do. My career is my future.

I feel I have a lot of freedom in this country. It may be dangerous, with rapists and murderers, but then so is every country in the world. I would like to spend time in India and Africa before I settle down. However, it can be a disadvantage not living in your country of origin. To be honest, I hardly ever speak Gujarati at home and I can't read or write it, even though I understand it well. I didn't take up the chance to go to classes and even though my parents teach me as much as they can, I think I've left it very late. I think living in India or Africa would mean that I would speak it more.

If I had lived in India, I imagine that I would be very different. My taste in clothing, people and hair-styles would have been different, for example. I probably would have long hair down to my upper thigh, rather than the shoulder-length style that I do have. My dress sense would be different too, but a lot of it would be influenced by the weather. I would still be interested in Indian music, but maybe I would be less in to English rock and dance music like I am now.

I've never visited Asia or Africa, but from my parents' experiences, I can tell that life is very hard there. I might not be able to get used to the lifestyle there. It is so different compared to simple Britain.

Even though the countries are beautiful and hot, it might take many years to settle down there. But if my parents could adapt to another country, then maybe I could do it too.

Harsha Dhokia

Is India Ready for Me?

My name is Shabneet Kaur Chadha and I am fifteen years old. I am a Kasadhari Sikh which means that I have kept my hair long and have never cut it. I was born and brought up in London and I am the oldest child in my family.

I'm not scared of being Asian nor am I ashamed of it. In fact, I'm utterly filled with joy at being Indian. What brought on this transformation, you may ask? It's not drugs, I'll tell you that now! I used to count myself as ordinary but it was my last trip to India that changed me. Let me explain.

Usually, when I went to India, I always enjoyed myself as it was great to go there on holiday. I loved seeing all my relatives, I loved going to the beach and playing outside our block of flats in the evenings with all the other children. I also enjoyed the mobile fairground rides I went on. The fact that you could get food on the roadside amazed me as I was always hungry! Not to forget the noisy rikshaws I adored. But there was a lot about India I hated, like how dirty and smelly it was! The roads weren't roads in my opinion and there were beggars everywhere. I hated it when it was too hot and the rain was hot and dirty. What got me most was that they couldn't cook English food properly! But that attitude soon changed.

In October 1994 I went to India for my youngest masi's wedding in Bombay. A masi is your mother's sister. My masi was having an arranged marriage, but she had had a say in who the groom would be. They had a ten-month engagement so that they could get to know each other. I met the groom and he definitely had a sense of humour and was good fun. The wedding was to be held in the gurudwara. A gurudwara is the Sikh place of worship and there are many in Bombay. There are quite a few functions before the actual wedding, like cocktail parties and hotel dinners and because this was the last wedding in my mother's family it was a pretty big affair. Relatives were coming from all over India and from abroad. When we all get together it's havoc! With so many functions we all need a new wardrobe. What a pity, we'll have to go shopping! Shopping is a major part of all weddings but especially Indian ones. People will spend anything from £60 to £1000 on an outfit and they're not even the bride! Ridiculous, in my opinion, but there's no harm in trying them on!

So, in the beginning, this trip wasn't very different from my other trips to India, which had also been for weddings. Like a lot of Indians in Britain, I thought India was a disgustingly dirty country, full of poor people, which made stupid films about men and women who fell in love every so often! However, on this trip, I learned to look beyond all that. It's like a pool; the surface can be deceptive. You have to look more closely to find its depth and I found India's depth. Believe me, it's deep!

Over there it was amazing. I loved it. I saw my culture in full swing. India is where I'm from; the wedding was just part of it. A Sikh wedding in India is a lot more fun because you're on home ground. You have the groom riding on a horse with his family dancing around him until they get to the gurudwara. Upstairs, the bride waits until everyone is settled and then the ceremony begins. My masi was very emotional. After the ceremonies and eating, everyone goes to the bride's house. From then on, it's water-works all the way, as everyone cries when the bride leaves her parental home to start a new life. The wedding just highlighted my culture and background – everything is a part of it – the slums, the smells and all the people. The wedding wasn't only symbolising a change in my masi's life, but in mine too.

Before this trip, I attended the gurudwara with my family most weeks, but it used to be more like a chore. I think that's because I didn't understand very much of what was being said, as I didn't know all that much Punjabi and so I found it boring. Because everything was in English at school, I didn't really want to learn Punjabi. It could also have been because I was too young to understand my religion. After going to

India, I felt ignorant compared to my cousins who could sing Punjabi hymns. In fact, I used to be forced to speak Punjabi at home, but I do it naturally now and I've even done a GCSE in it. When I was younger, I thought Punjabi was useless because it is English that is spoken and taught everywhere. In India I realised that I was wrong. I felt a part of the family more when I spoke in Punjabi or Hindi. Sometimes, something sounded stupid in English but fine in Punjabi or Hindi. These languages are a part of my culture and are different forms of communication which can't always be translated. I also actually listened to what was being said in the gurudwara when I went to India. The sounds and the tranquillity of the prayers were like a sanctuary from the busy, bustling lives outside. When I stopped and thought about it, I knew I wanted to keep being a part of all this. I began to take pride in my religion and going to the gurudwara while I was there, and have continued since I came back.

I always knew I would have an arranged marriage and I just accepted it, but as I grew older, I secretly began to question it. None of my other friends in London were going to have their husbands chosen for them nor were they restricted about making friends, especially those of the opposite sex. I knew about women who were just married off without a say in the matter and I also knew about women who ran off with their boyfriends and what was thought about them in the community. I didn't want to be either. My parents had always assured me that I would get the final decision in who I married and I trust that will happen. Seeing my masi's wedding reassured me that I could be happy if I had an arranged marriage.

Aspects of my life in London made me feel different – like going out on my own isn't allowed or staying over at a friend's house or even going on the tube. I've never actually had complete independence in London. But in India, I had a taste of freedom. My parents felt I was safe in India whereas here they don't. I was allowed out on my own, with and without cousins and friends. It felt great. I stayed in my nani and nanaji's (grandparents') house in Bombay with my mum and my two sisters as well as another masi and her two sons. My mamaji (mother's brother), his wife and two sons also lived there with my youngest masi. When the whole of our family was together it was great and when my mum's uncle also came along with his four children it was even better. There were fourteen children altogether and when we went out the traffic had to stop! I had the time of my life with them. I had family around me in London, but this was different. It wasn't the same as it was in India and I felt insecure when I got back to England.

Indian life was wonderful and caught me completely by surprise. Everywhere I looked, life was blooming and bursting forth. There was never a dull moment. I felt safe there. Nothing was boring. There were colours everywhere, even on the road, not just greens and concrete grey but colourful flowers and the brown earth beneath my sandals. You saw people from all walks of life dressed in different ways – in saris, suits, jeans, trousers, shorts, skirts – even rags were all in an array of colours. There were all kinds of smells, not all pleasant I'll admit! When I first came out of the airport my nostrils were polluted by the stench of rotting rubbish and sewage! Some welcome! But after a while, it became unnoticeable and it's better for you than London exhaust fumes! I had never expected to have such a good time. All the stereotypes and bad thoughts I had had were reversed. I was so overwhelmed by so many new good feelings that I ended up crying. Suddenly, I loved India and I wanted to stay there. I had once thought India could never be a part of me but now it was stuck to me.

I missed India a lot when I came back to London. Suddenly, it was London that was smelly, dull and depressing. It was such a contrast to the life I'd led in Bombay. It was as if I'd crawled out of my shell and a change had taken place deep inside me. I *wanted* to be Indian. I wanted to abide by my parents' wishes but have a mind of my own as well. I still wanted to go to university and have a career and get married to someone my parents liked but who I had picked. But my way of thinking, beliefs and views had changed. I no longer wanted to be the totally Westernised girl from London. I also wanted to be an Indian girl. In fact, what I really wanted was to be a bit of both. But what's a blend between the two? 'Englishness' is very different from being Indian and I didn't know how to act inbetween. Whose beliefs should I follow? I didn't want to keep changing my personality depending on whose company I was in. I wanted to change my way of thinking so that I could be someone *I* liked and I realised that this involves my culture, because my culture is a part of me and it makes me happy.

I know now that I am myself, Shabneet Kaur
Chadha, an individual, a liberated woman. I'd really
like to go back to India one day. I'm scared that I
might not be ready for India but also, will India be
ready for me?

Shabneet Chadha

Set Yourself Free

I don't know how to start to describe myself. I feel identity-less, but very unique. On paper, I'm 'Asian–Other', but in my head, I am a cocky little person with lots of aspirations, inspirations and ambition. Maybe a potted personal history would help to describe me.

My parents are East African, their parents are Indian; I was born in Wales. So, I was brought up by brown parents, with brown values, in a white middle-class community. I went to a white middle-class girls' private school and I had brown skin, short Western hair, Western clothes, Eastern name, Western friends. So . . . I guess I'm in an identity wasteland.

I used to insist that I was Welsh, rather than say that I was Indian or East African Asian or British or of Asian descent. It was easier to say Welsh, because there isn't a stereotype of a brown Welsh person. The only

Welsh connotations were to do with sheep – and I didn't mind the jokes which ensued about that. Now I will only agree to being *me*.

I have some fantasies of what I want – I want to be a doctor, I want to own a beach house, I want to listen to lots of laid-back music. I want to be loved by a wonderful guy, maybe have kids, but most of all I want to be blissfully contented. Cheesy stuff and I love it.

But, back on Earth, doing A levels is a bum, family can be a big bum, but the biggest bum is me, or maybe it's society at large, or maybe it's Asian-ness that's the biggest buttox-bottom of all.

NOT because of all the boring oppression-type issues associated with being Asian; it's true, racism *is* out there, but I don't want to use it as a crutch or an excuse. It's there, but hey, life's a bitch. The way I see it, by educating ourselves, by focusing on our dreams and busting a gut to get what we want, we will further ourselves and also make the West stand up and take notice. In this world money talks, sure, but I think that the intellect is taking over – which is no bad thing. I think people of colour should fight things that hold them back. Things like the archaic attitudes that still exist towards women; like racism, and the class system that still persists in Asian culture. But we should also be instilling values of hard work and self-esteem into the younger generations, showing them the beautiful parts of our culture, educating them in a secular and spiritual way and – I regard this to be the most important – teaching them that material pos-sessions are not a measure of status but rather that

49

integrity, humility, generosity, open-mindedness and love are what people should notice and respect.

I don't know how many other people think like me. I'm fortunate enough to have had the opportunity to be well educated, but that isn't the only thing that makes me think like I do. I think many of my peers look to their white equivalents and compare themselves, then feel short-changed in some way, or bitter that they are not the same. If you ask people if that's true, I doubt that they'll admit it, but I'm sure at some stage, they've felt like this. I know I have. But then, we should focus on what we *do* have; we should be proud that even though our ancestors suffered hardships, we are still emerging as a successful population. Our culture is so diverse, we have so many traditions and beliefs to draw on and learn from – we should make the most of it.

However, being Asian can be a downer (particularly for first generation Western–Asians), if you find it hard to reconcile the two parts of yourself – like I do. I'm not trying to forget my roots and be a 'white wannabee', but I've given up trying to be a race, and I'm trying to be an individual. I've found this difficult because the one thing that I can draw strength from (my family history, my heritage) can end up tearing me apart. For example, this gorgeous guy has just asked· me out and of course I said 'yes', because I've had a crush on him for ages. But, before I gave up being a race, I would have thought 'shit, I'm doing my A levels, my parents are barely letting me out, never mind letting me go out with a white bloke . . .' But I thought, I'm not missing out on Dave, so I said 'yes' to him. I was really worried about telling my parents – it was awful. But in the end, I just said that a friend had asked me out and I had said yes, was that okay? Mum asked if he was white and Dad gave me a few pearls of wisdom like not to do anything I'd regret, or make any commitments, because I might find someone else that I would want to spend the rest of my life with.

Being open, I think, is the best way of going about potentially volatile issues, because I think that it helps to strengthen respect in both parties. In the past, I would have said 'no' to Dave, thinking right from the beginning that it wouldn't work, but now I think that I can be happy with him. I think that I deserve to be happy. I'm just going to have to brace myself for when I do exams and won't be able to see him, but we'll see how it goes.

One thing that I'll never be able to get round, I think, is the 'study' versus 'going out' conflict. My parents can't seem to understand that I know what I'm doing. I know it's because they care that they hassle me to work; they know how much I want to be a doctor, but I'm a bit unlucky too, because I've got this cousin who is an absolute boffin – he went to Oxford, got a first – and they keep citing his example to me. I do try to ignore it, but it still gets my goat.

My other Asian problem, specific to a YFA (Young Female Asian, for those who don't know) is . . . body hair! Love it, hate it, plait it, bleach it, wax it, electrolyse it, do what you will, but being a YFA almost certainly means you're a walking jungle at some level. Forget family and personal relationships being a stumbling block for you, this, the dreaded sprout, is a far bigger problem. Summer is the worst time of year as you're dying of heat exhaustion, but you can't wear shorts and a vest as it requires a major waxing offensive before you look human! Forget any kind of sexual activity altogether – when you've finally found someone, you want to keep them, not scare them away!

I may sound as if I'm a few slices short of a loaf, but this is the first time that I feel in control of my life. I've had some tough things to deal with, like bulimia, but instead of taking the 'easy' way out (believe me, I know how tempting it is), I've kept going. I've got ambition and I'll be damned if I'm going to be unhappy. I got through things by having really, really good friends who helped me and by realising that there is so much out there in the world – the best bits are just there for the taking. We should actively search out happiness, love and adventures. We should travel and squeeze the last drop out of life. We should be out there doing the things that make the stories that you share with your best mate. Just because we are YFAs, it doesn't mean that we have a disadvantage or any less of a right to all the good bits in life. It might be a bit more difficult, but you can choose to wallow in problems and be self-pitying or you can choose to set yourself free.

That is probably the most liberating thing in the world – to go out there and really *live*. I realised that I was my own jailor; yes I might have body hair, a short weird body, a big nose and bad skin, but I'm also wise, strong and also more beautiful than I thought I could be. People say I have nice eyes and a good smile; some like my legs, others my bum.

It's really not all that bad being me. The best bit of me, I think, is my imagination and the fact that simple things – like bear hugs! – make me happy. Overall, life is positive; being a YFA can be positive. As I get older, being brown is getting better, so my advice to any other young brown female would be, whatever your race, go out there and *live*. DON'T let race, sex, family or body hair get in your way, coz you're all beautiful!

Salima Dhalla

Coming Out

As far as I'm concerned, I've been a lesbian since I was born. But as far as feelings are concerned and when I first became aware of it, it was at an early age, about seven, I think. I went to a girls' school, back home in Pakistan, and I was attracted to Miss Zeenat and to some of the older girls. But of course, it never occurred to me that this was a sexual feeling. At that age, I didn't know anything.

Mine was a girls' school and there was a boys' school across the road. I first really noticed that I was different when my older sisters and older girls from school got excited about meeting the boys and about getting love letters from them. I knew that was not what I wanted. I knew that the crushes I had were what the other girls were feeling for boys. When I wrote poems for myself or sang Indian love songs, it was another girl I imagined, not a boy. Indian movies showed men and women falling in love. I was always imagining myself in the male role. But I didn't know what I was; I didn't know I was a lesbian – I didn't know what to call it.

I came to Britain when I was ten, because one of my older sisters was ill. She needed a heart operation. My father was here anyway, working and sending money back to Pakistan. So, my mother and four sisters came here (I'm the youngest), while two sisters and a brother stayed behind. They were already married and settled in Pakistan, so did not need to come over. I couldn't speak a word of English and had to have extra lessons. Classmates thought I was backward and would laugh and whisper about me behind my back. When I reported this to the teacher, he just laughed at me and said that if I couldn't speak English, how did I know that they were talking about me? When I told my mum, she tried to get my dad to go in and complain, because he could speak English, but he never did.

This junior school was mixed, girls and boys, and I had a crush on a white music teacher almost right away. I would feel jealous when she talked to male teachers. I made friends with white girls who were tomboy types (maybe they're gay too now?). So, as well as not being able to speak English, I also had these feelings, which I couldn't tell anyone about. It was like being doubly different.

Then I started at a girls' secondary school. My feelings for women grew stronger and I started to fancy the sixth formers. When my other friends were playing, I started to hang round the sixth form block.

55

I never managed to speak to the sixth formers, I just admired them from a distance! My friends began to realise something was happening when I kept talking about catching a glimpse of a particular girl. That's when they asked me if I was a lesbian, and that's the first time I learned a word for it. So other people had to tell me what it was and explain it to me. Actually, I didn't admit it to them, because I knew that it was going to make me more different from them, but I sort of acknowledged it to myself.

I didn't do anything about it or tell anyone – I am a strict Sunni Muslim and I thought it was a phase that would just go away. I thought that I was the only one – I thought it was a really bad sickness that I had. I'd had a religious upbringing and that was what I had been taught. So I just repressed it. I had crushes on women but didn't do anything about them.

I actually came out to my mum just recently, after my eighteenth birthday, because I couldn't lead a straight life any more. My dad had died already, and that made it easier to tell my mum. I knew it would have been worse if my dad had been alive. He was the sort of person who wouldn't just say he'd kill me, he'd do it.

My mum also thought it was a phase that I would grow out of. I was in college by then and that's when I started to rebel. I cut off my hair to look modern, wore jeans and bought trainers. She was shocked. I think trying to be free like this was a way of expressing my sexuality; I was being what I wanted to be. Mum thought I was trying to be a man. Then I discovered gay groups and realised that I wasn't the only one.

Mum kept denying I was a lesbian; she said it was the influence of white people at college.

Coming out to her was very painful for me. Even though it had taken me years to admit it to myself, I was now confident about what I was. But it was still very emotional telling my mother. She still thinks it's a white woman's disease and if I had been in Pakistan, this would never have happened; that it's this country that has corrupted me. What she doesn't know is that in the long holidays back in Pakistan, I had a girlfriend, who was the first person to kiss me! We grew up together and I did have feelings for her, but at the time I didn't admit them to myself. It was at a family gathering and lots of people were staying in the house. All the beds and rooms were divided up between the guests, and as we were such good friends, we shared a single mattress in a room with all the other children that we had to keep an eye on. It was hot, and I only had my shalwar on. She had her shalwar and kurta on. We were lying facing each other and she started to kiss and touch me. I was a bit shocked that she made the first move; after all, I was the one that had been in England, where this sort of thing happened.

I think that in an Islamic country, things *do* go on, but they call it something else and deny what it really is.

After I came out to Mum, she told my uncles who began to get very strict with me and said that I must stop being gay. They said that if it had been anything else that was wrong with me, like I was going out with an African man, or I was pregnant, they would help me by saying the right prayers for forgiveness. But being gay was the worst thing. They began to talk about making me get married to a Pakistani man to 'cure' me. I got scared and I left home. Now I'm in a hostel and this is where I met Sally, my first real girlfriend.

One evening, she invited me for dinner. She had cooked pasta, which I had never had before and I didn't think I would like it. But I tried it and it was nice. She was being really lovely. We were sitting in a lounge, which was shared, but nobody else was using it at the time. I was feeling much calmer than I had been for ages. Just as we finished eating, some people walked in, so Sally suggested that we go to her room and have coffee. We went up and she lit some perfumed candles and put on some music. There was a graveyard outside her window and the sun was setting so it was a bit scary-looking outside. We sat on the floor, leaning against the bed. It was really cosy with lots of cushions and arty things she had made herself. I hadn't been so happy for such a long time. She read some of her poems to me, but some of the English was still difficult for me to understand. We had a cigarette, still talking and sipping drinks, and then there was a pause and that was it, she kissed me and I felt like I was in love and, for the very first time, that everything was going to be okay.

Sally was wonderful. She was really supportive to me. I was upset about leaving home and losing my family, and she really looked after me. She let me cry all the time! She was also 'coming out' about her sexuality – she thought she was bi-sexual. She was white, six years older than me, had sandy hair and was studying sociology. We didn't have a lot in common, but we were looking after each other.

I'm still hiding from my family. My mum is back in Pakistan and I'm only in contact with her by letter. She has the address of a friend of mine, who forwards post to me. In every letter she writes, she hopes that I will now be straight. They have tried to find me and force me to go back with them, so I have to be careful, even though I really love and miss my mum.

In the meantime, I've got Sally and her friends as my new family. I have also met Asian lesbians who are now my family too, so I hope that it will work out for me.

Leila

A Festive Affair

Religious festivals are always circled in all Hindu calendars. When I was younger I always accompanied my parents on their weekly visits to the temple. I found this very exciting and adventurous as a young child. I could run around the temple and ring all the large bells at the entrance. Often the priest would give me sweets or 'prasad' (holy offerings made to the Gods). The temple is the central meeting point for the Hindu community to congregate, catch up on the latest gossip and celebrate the many festivals which occur throughout the year.

My favourite festival was Navarati. It is held to commemorate the mythic battle between Goddess Durga and the monstrous demon Mysasawre, who was causing havoc to the peace and serenity of India. It was a battle between good and evil which lasted nine days and nine nights. It was Goddess Durga who eventually victoriously slayed the demon, and the festival lasts nine days to reflect the length of the battle.

I always knew that Navarati was due when the leaves began to fall from the trees in autumn. This festival is normally celebrated during October or November. As a young girl I couldn't wait until my nine days of fun could begin. I looked forward to dressing up in different Indian outfits, complete with bangles, necklaces and a bright bindi (a spot normally worn above the eyebrows). I was also allowed to wear my mum's lipstick. I felt like a princess in my glittery and sparkly costume, but unfortunately I think I probably resembled an overdone Christmas tree.

As the years passed, I was no longer a 'wannabe princess'; I had finally become a teenager who was more interested in attending the disco at the local youth club for a bop than going to the temple. Most Asian teenagers were not as fortunate as I was because my parents allowed me to go out whenever I wanted, as long as the neighbours did not see me entering the house late at night. For many others, Navarati was the only time in the year they could have a social life.

Navarati was more like a disco for repressed and downtrodden Hindu teenagers than a religious festival. Many girls would have to be at the beck and call of their parents every day and night. However, during these nine days, they could dance all night. I should explain that by dancing I am not referring to disco-dancing, I mean Indian dancing. The dancing was done around the shrine of the Goddess Durga at the temple. Two circles are formed around the altar, the outer circle is composed of the older 'Aunties' who thud around the altar clapping their hands to the beats of the music. The inner circle is where the young, stylish and 'hard-core' dancers whizz around the Goddess Durga clicking their fingers while twisting and turning to the music. I soon realised that I had two left feet when it came to the complicated footsteps of Indian dancing. Before my mother dragged us to the temple I would always warn her that I did not want her to force me to dance. She always managed to drag me around the slow lane with the other Aunties where I would walk around the altar, a few steps at a time whilst clapping. It may sound easy but the dance floor was slippery and unsafe due to all the cheesy bare feet which left trails of sweaty slime on the floor. I felt like I was trying to roller-skate on black ice.

Dancing was not made easier by the hindrance of wearing a heavy silk sari. The waistband was so tight that even I had a bulge of what looked like fat resting on the top of my skirt, and I'm considered very slim! As you can imagine, I could hardly breathe let alone dance. But I had to carry on waltzing around the shrine since my mum had ordered me to be on my best behaviour. This meant that I was not allowed to complain in front of the Aunties. I had to behave like the perfect and obedient Indian girl because the Aunties were always hunting for scandal to spread. This was the perfect opportunity for the gossipy ringleaders to exchange useful pieces of tittle-tattle, especially about misbehaving girls. This could lead to the assumption that the girl was not worthy of introduction into the marriage market.

This is every Asian parent's nightmare. It seems that having a worthy marriage partner is a goal which all parents strive for on behalf of their children. This usually meant that I would have a swotty, nerdish-looking young suitor who was normally an accountant, drove a BMW and had no social life or personality! This was the sort of dull and stale life my parents wanted for me. I did not want to think about marriage. I was quite happy being young, free and single. Single girls like me were a rare breed in the Indian community since most of them had no social life and were desperate to unleash all their pent-up sexual frustrations. I felt it was disgusting that Navarati had become a 'meat market' for teenagers. The festival had lost its religious significance and the toilets were the central pulling place. It was here that the illicit affairs would blossom. The lads usually lurked in the dark corners. I always thought that this was to hide their greasy, acne-covered faces and pubescent bodies. I could not see the attraction of trying to seduce a puny and unmasculine wimp. I thought the Aunties were more manly! However, the other Hindu girls had a totally different opinion. I had never seen such a cluster of made-up faces in all my life. All I could see were red blobs of lipstick in the distance on the white canvas faces. It always amazed me that Indian girls wore foundation that was two shades lighter than their skin, to conjure up the image of having fair skin (it is a universally known fact in Indian society that fair skin is an indication of beauty).

I discovered that the girls would leave the dance floor and stroll to the toilets to attract the attention of the opposite sex. No words would be spoken – nobody wanted to be seen chatting to the boys because the results could be disastrous; it could spark off the chain of gossipy Aunties to spread some slander. The seduction game was played by the girls who glanced at the lads and, if one smiled, the girl had struck lucky. It was then time to sneak outside to the car park to arrange a date. This was usually set for a lunchtime when their parents would be out at work.

I was not drawn in to developing any dangerous liaisons at the temple or trying to attempt to dance with my unco-ordinated dance steps. I always sat hiding amongst the Aunties waiting for my mum to stop dancing. I was sitting by myself because I no longer had any Indian friends. I had moved schools and my peer group was from an English background. I had a free and unrestrictive life, unlike most of the other girls who had to cherish every moment for the next nine days. Navarati was still a religious festival for me, although I couldn't wait to get home, take off my sari and jump into my comfortable tracksuit.

Kalpna Patel

An Educated Girl

Growing up in Britain and being brought up in two cultures, the Bengali and the English, has made me deal with a lot of things ranging from racism to living up to the expectation of what a good Bengali girl is. However, these themes occur in every British Bengali girl's life. Unfortunately, I think these are issues that we will have to deal with continually, as will our daughters, until our community accepts that we as individuals are influenced by both cultures and that's what makes us who we are.

But I'm even more different. The fact that I wanted to study and eventually gain a degree has been one long controversy for me and my family. The main reason my education is such a big issue is that my parent's duty was, supposedly, to provide me with a Muslim education, keep me in the English schooling system until legally required and, at sixteen, choose a decent man for me to be happily married to. I think my uncle summed up the attitude of the majority of people around us when he said to my mother, 'Allah has blessed you with many daughters so that you can help bring the poor Bengali boys over to this country.' My mother replied, 'No, the reason Allah blessed us with girls is because He knew we would look after them properly and not just use them as charity.'

Because my parents had been brought up in this atmosphere, I assumed they didn't expect much of me. Therefore, I was quite content in primary school and early secondary school because I thought nobody was watching me. I thought they had my future planned already. All I was concerned with at the time was the fact that I hardly knew how to speak English, let alone read and write, so I was too busy concentrating on that to worry about anything else.

At school, I had been dragging my dad off to all the parent evenings, but I didn't think he was paying attention to any of my teachers. I should have realised there was a change in his attitude when I was instructed to copy out pages and pages of handwriting so that my handwriting would improve, while all the other eight- and nine-year-olds played outside. It wasn't until I was fifteen years old that I found out why my parents had begun to push me so much. They said it was because they realised that I had 'potential'. What was also interesting was that both my parents had studied in Bangladesh and had wanted to carry on in their studies but were forced to stop. Dad had to leave and mum had to stop because everything was a mess during the conflict between Bangladesh and Pakistan. It was during these early years of secondary school that I really felt my parents' support for the first time. I often think that they are living their hopes and dreams through me, but they are also giving me the chance of gaining a secure future.

It wasn't until I joined the Duke of Edinburgh's Award Scheme in my third year that the comments from my relatives really got under way. It was like everyone had launched this personal war on me and my family. I understood that they found it strange that I wanted to get into higher education, since none of their own daughters seemed to have any ambition. It would have been nice to think that they talked about me going off to expeditions because they were concerned or interested, but instead, I found out it was because they didn't trust a girl by herself and thought my parents were stupid for letting me go. Throughout secondary school, my dad was continuously being told about numerous 'really good boys' and what good husbands they would make. My dad was not listening to any of it. The problem with me and my relatives is that neither side can really state their true feelings about each other. I've been brought up to respect my elders, so I can never say 'please don't be ridiculous' – well, not to their faces. On the other hand, they can't start a really heated debate about what they dislike about me studying, because my parents would show them the door. Still, my aunt didn't win any popularity contests when she told everyone that I was turning into a Christian and was losing my way. This was after seeing me studying, wearing jeans and a baggy top. As far as she was concerned, I should be wearing a shalwar kameez and socialising with her when she comes round, no matter what assignments have to be handed in. My other favourite comment from her was, 'With all this studying you let her do, she still won't learn anything,' by which she meant cooking, cleaning and taking care of a husband.

As far as I was concerned, getting an education was no big deal. I wasn't doing anything special. Besides, I saw hundreds of people at school doing exactly the same thing as me. It didn't hit me until the fifth year at secondary school. I was interviewing people on careers and why it was sometimes a big issue for certain people. I asked a Bengali girl, 'So, if you could have any job what would it be?' She replied that she would like to work as a check-out assistant, and many other Bengali girls came out with similar answers. The fact is that their answers didn't reflect their dreams and ambitions, but the restrictions placed on them. They know these are the only kind of jobs they would be allowed to do without causing conflict between them and their parents. It was at that time that I realised how fortunate I was to have the parents I have.

College was different, because I finally met other Bengali girls that had ambitions similar to mine. This meant I was no longer the odd one out. I had been silly to think that once my relatives found out about these college girls they would back off. They didn't. They never grasped the fact that all I wanted to do was be me, and all I wanted to know was why was it such a crime to want to learn and succeed? Even today, it is an obvious fact that boys wouldn't be treated so harshly for having ambitions.

What inevitably happened was that I didn't trust anyone outside my immediate family. It made me angry that they sneered at me and talked about what a lousy job my parents had done in bringing me up. They still got on my nerves by saying, 'It doesn't matter what you do, you will never be English'. They are wrong in thinking that I was abandoning my culture or my background. I know I'm Bengali and I'm not ashamed of it. I know the adult thing to do was to just ignore their comments, but I couldn't help getting worked up about it. The more they said I dressed in Western clothes, the more I did it. The strange thing is that I actually thrived on their comments, because the more they hated what I did, the more determined I was to do well. I've always had this sense that I would be okay despite all the 'she's going to fail' speeches.

Now that I have got into university to study law, the relatives still haven't stopped. I now have everyone waiting and watching for my next move or mistake and I hate it. If I do badly, or even if I pass and don't get a good job, I know what the consequences will be. I'll have all those relatives telling my parents 'I told you so – what's the point of putting her through education when she can't get a high-paying job?' My parents will be humiliated. But worst of all, I would feel thoroughly ashamed of myself. When I finish university, I'll have set the standard for everyone else in my family. But despite everything, I'm glad that it's given my sisters and brother the opportunity to see that university is not something remote and unobtainable in their lives.

My battle to get myself educated won't ever really end. I guess I did something out of the ordinary where my relatives are concerned and maybe their dislike of me isn't because I'm studying, but because I never really followed their instructions or tried to fulfil their expectations. I'll just have to live with it. I know that I am a very ambitious and determined person. I am prepared to work hard to achieve what I can. Most importantly, I want people to realise that even though both cultures have influenced me, I am Bengali first and foremost and I value our customs and traditions a lot more than I am given credit for. I want my parents to know that in their house, I am what I believe a good Bengali girl is and I respect the way they have brought me up.

Nina Miah

I Don't Look Like One

I am a practising Shia Muslim, but everybody I meet says that I don't look like one. I've got long hair and I wear glasses (I'm too lazy to wear my contact lenses) and I wear jeans and trainers all the time. Maybe that's it, maybe you don't get Muslim tomboys.

My family is East African Asian, and a lot of this community lives around us. My parents are quite liberal: they have quite a personal way of practising Islam, so apart from calling me at Uni to check if I'm saying my prayers, they're all right. I wish I'd taken a year off before coming here though: A levels were really hard and I only just got the grades to come here, so I feel I need a rest. But also, it's a bit of a shock leaving home and budgeting on my grant and having all these choices without being told what to do. A year off might have given me some space to get gradually more independent, maybe even get a job, although my dad probably wouldn't have let me. My parents wanted me to choose a university in my home town, so I could stay at home for my degree. They said that the only reason a girl leaves home is to get married. What would people think! It was a battle to get them to allow me to try other places. Finally, I had to argue that this place had the best course and the best reputation – that worked! This place is a good compromise, as it's not too far away. They get to feel that I'm close enough and accessible, and I get my freedom.

I don't know if I'll go to mosque much while I'm here though. I went once, in Fresher's Week, and everyone there seemed really friendly. They offered me lifts to and from campus to make it easier for me to attend, but it's really hard to choose mosque when everyone else is at the Union bar or at a party, having a good time. I really feel like I'm missing out when I don't go out with my friends.

Drinking, smoking, drugs, and sex before marriage are not allowed – I'm not sure which rules are Islamic, which are cultural and which are Mum and Dad. I do know Muslims in my community who do all of these things, but mostly it's men, not girls.

I think I might try a cigarette, just one, and taste a sip of something alcoholic (I'm not sure what), just so I know what it's like. I once kissed someone who smoked though, and it was really awful. Another thing that puts me off is that when I go to the Union bar, it's so smoky that it makes my eyes water. I hate coming out stinking as well, even though it doesn't seem to bother my friends.

Drinking used to be more appealing, before I came to Uni. Even in the first few weeks, I was helping people to get back to Halls, because they had drunk too much and didn't know what they were doing. I would bring them water to try to sober them up, so that they wouldn't be ill, or I would help them in the toilet if they were sick. I worry that if I try it and I like it, I might drink too much and end up like them!

I'm not going to have sex. Mum and Dad want me to marry a Muslim boy from our community, and I think that's right, because culture and religion are two very important things to have in common.

I had boyfriends before I came to Uni. Mum says she always prefers it if I bring them home, so she doesn't have to worry about where I am at night. They have mostly been from my community, but I think Mum thinks that I only hold hands with them and don't do anything else, like kiss.

I do wonder what my Mum and Dad would say if they knew I was thinking like this. They think I don't do these things because I'm *told* not to; they don't know how curious I am about them. I thought it would be harder to say 'no' to things like alcohol when I came to university; I thought people would think I was weird when I said that it was against my religion, but because I always asked for a coke or lemonade right from the start, everybody's used to it and nobody pressures me.

In fact, I was at an Asian party once, before Uni; one of the boys asked me if I wanted a drink, so I asked for a coke. He said 'go on, have something stronger' so I explained that I was a Muslim and didn't drink. When he came back, I tried the drink and it tasted funny. He said he had put rum in it, so I would have a good time! I was really angry with him and never went out with his group again. At Uni, the boys are more mature than this and they're all white.

There is an Asian Society, but they're really cliquey. The girls just want to dress up all flashy and the boys go around telling in-jokes and bitching – I'm not interested in either. I thought I would feel closer to them because they're Asian like me, but actually, they're into all the 'vices' just like everyone else. Maybe it's because it's my religion that's making me feel separate, rather than being Asian. On the other hand, there *are* practising Muslims on campus, but they're all Sunni Malaysians, so we have even less in common!

I think Mum and Dad will like the friends I've made – I'm planning to live with them in a house next year. That will be a whole new battle, because they're all white, except for one girl who is mixed-race Asian, and two of them are *boys*! But I trust all of them, because they have never laughed at me or asked too many nosy stupid questions about going to mosque. They keep bacon away from me in the fridge and in fact, one of the boys has a car and has given me lifts to the bus stop to make it easier for me to go to mosque! I've started to introduce them to my parents, so Mum and Dad will see that they come from 'good homes'.

But I think that I will stick with Islam because when things happen, I always have my faith to keep me going. For example, when I was coming to university, my mum was away. I didn't know what to do – what to pack, what to wear — I wasn't even sure how I would get there, because my dad was going to work. When I did finally arrive by myself, lugging my single suitcase, I saw that everybody else's parents had brought car loads of stuff — even stereos, irons, toasters and kettles. I felt really lonely then, and that's when I found out where the mosque was and went. I felt much better. And, at other times, like when my granny died, I was so sad, because she was really ill and I was helping to look after her at home and I watched as she passed away. I didn't know how I knew she had died, I just did, so I called everybody and they said yes, she'd died. I went to mosque a lot then, because it helped me to not be so sad. It made me feel like someone was listening to me and I began to feel stronger. But it's not only when things are bad; sometimes, when things go really well, like I get good grades, I go to mosque to say 'thank you' (especially because I usually go to ask for good grades first!).

So, I'm looking forward to the next couple of years and to getting my degree. I think I will become a different person, but I'll still be a Muslim, even at Uni, even though I don't look like one.

Farah Aly

Too Precious to be Put Last

What I thought was going to be a regular sleep-over with videos, chocolate and gossip turned out to be a night that changed me completely.

I was twelve and staying at my friend Munira's house. Our families had known each other since we were five years old. Her mum and older brother Abdul used to 'babysit' a group of us. The entire friendship was based on trust — as any good relationship should be.

On this particular evening, there were three girls, feasting on good films and gossip, when Abdul came in and started showing us some of his photos himself. He was eighteen, six foot tall and heavily built, and the pictures were of him messing about on his last day at school. The video we had been watching ended, so we all went upstairs to his room to choose another one. As we pored over video cases, he took out even more photos to show us. I indulged him by looking, to be polite; he had, after all, looked after me and the others countless times. He had pretty much seen me grow up and was like a big cousin brother really.

The next thing I knew, the others had left his room and he bolted the door, locking me in with him. I said I wanted to go and be with the others, but he sat me down in his chair and started to talk to me. He was saying things like 'Oh, you don't look your age,' and 'I'd be proud to walk down the street with you.' I didn't quite understand, but was feeling majorly uncomfortable with the situation, so I got up to leave. He got up to follow me, grabbed both my arms and pushed me on to his bed.

Instinctively, I drew my knees up to my chin to protect myself and crossed my legs, but it was useless. He prised my legs apart and put his head between them and started to touch me all over. I was completely scared and felt sick. I kept saying 'No, get off!' repeatedly and tried to put him off, but he was too heavy and just kept going. I seemed to freeze – I felt paralysed. My mind seemed to just switch off so that I didn't have to deal with what was happening. I hate admitting that I went into this kind of 'shut down', because I feel that I should have been able to do something to stop him, but I was totally scared. I didn't ask for it, I was petrified and my mind went blank.

The next thing I remember was him talking again, but it was different this time. This was probably the worst part and I hate thinking about it. This is the first time I have told anyone this, so here goes. He forced me to tell him my measurements and describe my underwear to him and he bit my breast, really hard. I didn't know what he would do to me if I didn't do as he said. He made me listen to him describe what he wanted to do to me sexually and then he got pictures of naked women out from under his bed. One was a cartoon of a woman with black hair, sitting on the edge of a bed, bleeding; he said that this would be me if I wasn't careful. I started to retch and he smiled and said that I shouldn't worry, he wouldn't hurt me. He began to take his shorts off, and this finally left my arms free to pull his head away from me by his hair and unbolt the door. Munira's room was next door, and as I went in, I realised they were already asleep. I got into bed and he blew me a kiss, saying 'next time' and smiled.

I didn't sleep, I didn't cry, I didn't move. I felt like I wasn't there at all. That night, I felt like the little girl that I had been began to die.

I carried on as if everything was normal for the next two years, keeping what had happened deeply buried. I didn't face it because I couldn't. I hated myself and began to think that it might have been my fault. I was ashamed of what had happened to me, so I didn't speak up. I felt physically sick just thinking about it.

Then, when I was fourteen, things started to go wrong. I was feeling tired and stressed out all the time and one day, we were at a religious festival and I just started to cry. When we got home, my mum prised it out of me, and I re-lived the whole thing again.

It felt surreal telling Mum. It was like a really bad B-movie; Mum shouted 'No, no!' and couldn't look me in the face. I couldn't handle that and started to cry. At this point, Mum asked me flatly if he had had intercourse with me. When I replied no, she said that it had been my own fault and walked out.

From that day, I went into shut-down mode again. I dressed like a boy, in baggy jeans and tops and passed myself off as an overconfident tomboy type. I did well at school, organising things and had lots of friends. But a part of me was still paralysed and trying to cope. I was confused – should I just try to act normally and get on with my life or stop and deal with it? It felt easier to just get on with it, but slowly, it got harder to keep up the front and I began to fall to pieces. I became quiet and withdrawn and stopped going out at all. I was sixteen.

One night, friends nagged me into going to a club with them, so I went. Towards the end of the evening, this guy started to get a bit over friendly and I froze again. He didn't do anything wrong really, but suddenly, everything got triggered off and I was scared again.

I isolated myself from my friends and shut everyone out – I thought I had to deal with it all myself. I still felt ashamed and couldn't tell anyone. I ended up losing the best friendship I have ever had, as I didn't feel able to confide in her. I also felt like I would be stopping her from having a good time if I burdened her with my problems. Maybe if my mum's response had been different, it would have encouraged me to talk to other people about it.

I was trying to deal with it all in my head, by myself. It was tense at home, so I put all my energy into school work, but that just made me tired. I felt really lonely. I don't know why, but I started to binge and then use laxatives and my self-esteem got worse.

About eighteen months ago, it was assembly time at school and someone was pestering me about something or other. I just lost it. I burst into tears and ran to the toilets, locking myself in. Some classmates came to find me and took me to see a teacher, who was really nice and arranged for me to see the school doctor.

The doctor didn't help at all. She acted like she was on some American chat show. She suggested family counselling, discussing the whole thing with my dad, and me coming to terms with my own sexuality. She didn't take my Asian background into account even once. I tried to explain that Asian girls aren't meant to even have a sexuality, much less express it! I tried to explain that it wasn't the 'done thing' to even talk in our family – we are all much better at pretending that nothing's going on!

I went home and tried talking to Mum about it once more. She had had over three years to deal with it herself, but when I said I wanted to see a counsellor, she said, 'Then everyone will know that there's something wrong with you.' She told me to drink holy water and pray every night. She was almost as good as the school doctor.

So, this is the reality; in the Asian community, abuse does happen, but it's such a taboo subject itself, that even getting help to deal with it is taboo.

I was lucky enough recently to make some brilliant new friends who listened to me – I feel like I owe them my life. I am still abusing laxatives and I went through a bit of an alcoholic patch, but my friends have been there for me.

You must be thinking that I'm a bit of a psycho, but I think I'm making progress now. No more booze for me. I'm less nervous about everything, a bit more confident and I'm even beginning to make friends with boys, although I don't go out with them. I am starting to get on better with my family and I hope to be applying to medical school after A levels.

The hardest thing has been living with myself. I've started to accept and stopped hating myself, so that I can get on with my life. I am still nervous about going to see a counsellor, because I feel like I don't want to go through it all again, even if it's good for me. I think at some level, I don't want to admit that I can't cope on my own. I have always had to be self-sufficient and cope with everything by myself, even before this happened. But, if I had to advise anyone else who has been through something similar, I would say deal with it right away, even if it means talking to a more distant relative or a teacher. People who are outside of your community are sometimes safer, as they don't judge you.

I wish that I had gone to see a counsellor as soon as possible and I wish I hadn't cut off from some really good friends. I wish there was more education and awareness in Asian communities, so that my family could have helped me, rather than see it as a stigma on themselves.

If it happens to you, you don't have to be on your

own and worry about what people will think – you're too precious to be put last.

P.S. I saw Abdul the other day when I went to visit Munira and I looked him right in the eye. He was visibly uncomfortable and had to leave his own house. That's how it should have been all along, the shame and guilt were his, not mine.

Rahila Punjwani

A Ugandan Indian in Britain

I am a fifteen-year-old Gujarati-speaking girl, practising the Hindu religion. My family is originally from India, but both my parents were born in Uganda, Africa. They were educated in Africa until the age of sixteen, and from there, they went to colleges in India. My grandparents had to work very hard to send money to their children, especially for my father, as he was one of eight. Times could be very hard for them sometimes. The whole family had to leave Uganda as the Prime Minister, Idi Amin, forced all Asians to pack-up and go in only ninety days. This was when my family came to England, as Uganda had been a British colony and they had British passports. My grandparents were not able to accept having to move, as they were losing their home and business. When they first moved to London they found it quite hard to fit in, but once they got used to the Western way of life they settled in quite well. I was born here, and living here is great, but I do want to find out more about the history of my family, their past way of life and generally how different life was for them compared to my brother and I.

My parents brought me up to be a practising Hindu, but did not impose it on me. I am not obliged to follow it just because they do. I am proud of my religion, because following a religion makes me feel secure; it is something that I feel strongly, and it's important to me. Although I am not very religious, I try to go to the temple occasionally, but I do not think it is necessary to go to temple in order to understand the religion. I think religion is about how much a person wants to know; I see it as a guide to my life. It is hard for some people to practise their religion in Britain, as there are not as many temples or mosques as there should be.

It can be very interesting living in Britain, as I am living in two cultures and this means that I have two groups of friends to go out with. One group is all Indian and we meet at various functions, the other group is a mixture of friends from school, who are all of different nationalities. I usually meet this group on weekends or holidays and go out shopping or to the cinema. We generally choose to go somewhere where we know all of us are allowed to go. I like knowing people from different ethnicities and backgrounds. I feel it is very important to learn about other cultures and religions and to respect them, as I would expect others to respect the culture and religion I follow.

I sometimes find myself wondering whether I actually fit in with the Western way of life, as my idea of socialising is not going to clubs and drinking. I would prefer to invite friends home or to meet up and go out for dinner. I know that to a certain extent, living in the West has influenced the way I think. For example, for a girl to be having a boyfriend at a young age does not really matter to me, whereas if I lived in India, I am sure that I would feel very differently. My parents would not accept me going out with a boy at this age, because they feel that my education should come first. I agree with them, as they are only trying to help me build a better future for myself. I do not mind my friends having boyfriends – it is their choice and does not really affect me.

One question that I am frequently asked in school when I say that I am Indian is 'Are you going to have an arranged marriage?' My answer is this – *only* if I ask for one. I would like to make it very clear that the term 'arranged marriage' does not mean that a boy and a girl meet once and if both their parents agree, they get married. In fact, for my community, all it means is that parents arrange for their children to meet, and if they like each other, they date. My friends are very curious, always asking questions about Indian weddings and what our various festivals and ceremonies are like.

Being Indian, we live as an extended family unit. All my relatives live near us and we are very close. My cousins and I are like friends, as we are of similar ages and we can relate to each other easily. I think it is nice to know all the family, despite the little arguments that go on, but that's normal in all families. The most important thing is that when one of us is in trouble or needs advice, we know we can rely on each other for help.

I have never really suffered any form of bullying due to being Indian and I feel quite lucky, as many of my Asian friends have been bullied because of it. There is one thing that annoys me a lot, even more than bullying, and that is racism. I do not know what pleasure people get out of being racist, putting others down just for coming from a different background. I was once called a 'paki' when I was in primary school and it really upset me. I felt that I didn't belong and that I was too different from everyone. It was only when my mother sat me down and explained that I should not have taken the remark to heart, that I should not pay attention to these people who make racist comments, that I felt better. If I was to come across someone being racist now I would still take my mother's advice and ignore them, as I see these people as being small-minded. I am still not prepared to accept racism, because it is not just one of those things that can be looked over. I sometimes wish people would wake up and realise that no matter what a person's skin colour, background or ethnicity, at the end of the day, everyone is human. This is a factor which should help us get on with each other; it is a shame that it has not worked so far.

My ambitions for the future are to go to university, get a good career and hopefully go back to India to learn more about my culture and about my roots. I have only been to India once before, and I would also like to visit Uganda, now that Asians are allowed back there. My main aim in life is to work hard and travel the world, so I can see how countries and people vary. I am sure that there are many different cultures and religions; I probably haven't even heard of some of them yet.

Overall, being Indian and living in this country is a real experience. I like living here and feel that this country has a lot to offer young people of my age. I have noticed that when it comes to thinking about this country, it is a lot better than some other places when it comes to issues like racism, as other places, like America, can be even worse.

I see growing up in Britain as an advantage for me, as the education system here is good and I hope this will give me a head start into a profession. The thing I like most about living here has to be knowing that I am secure and the worst has to be the unpredictable weather!

Niksha Thakrar

A Little Bit Normal

'Can I introduce you to Krishna?'

I've always wanted to say that. What a great question. You know, like 'Can I put you in touch with Jesus? Or Jehovah?' Or something.

Sometimes it can be really funny, but most of the time I feel insulted when somebody tries to perform a conversion. In my opinion, they've got to believe that theirs is better than mine. Just for the record, I also feel pretty annoyed and embarrassed if somebody tries to convert someone else to my religion, Hinduism. What a cheek!

I once read in a religious studies lesson that all Hindus have a shrine to the gods in their homes. I'd never spotted one in ours. I've since come across what must be the closest thing to it. It's a shelf on the mantelpiece with three papier mâché thingies on it, one of Shiva, one of Buddha, and one of Jesus. I suppose we're hedging our bets.

I am disabled and an only child. That probably says it all. I've been a little overprotected, often to the point of embarrassment. Mum and Dad, particularly Dad, tend to forbid me to do things, like ride my bike in a big group in a place I don't know. That may be okay when you're thirteen, but not when you're seventeen. The problem is dealing with that unnecessary interference whilst trying to be seen as a mature person, who is in control of your life. Apart from that, it makes you feel totally stupid.

I've had a comfortable childhood. I mean, I've never been denied anything that I really needed. We're not rich, but we're okay for money, and like many dads, mine is a pushover when it comes to his 'little princess'. However, I've also spent a lot of my childhood being told what I will and will not be 'able to manage dear', when the only person who could tell me that is me. I don't like other people telling me what's best for me, who does? I know that horrible feeling you get when people make assumptions about your capabilities and then publicly prevent you from doing something. This gives me permission to get angry and tell people about it because nobody else knows how annoying it is. I think I'm a lot sharper for the experience, and certainly wiser.

Thousands of disabled people, particularly Asian disabled people, have their lives dominated by Ma and Pa. I'm lucky. My parents are comparatively good at the 'right to my own life' thing. I think they've been worried about me, more than anything else: What will she do for money? Will she get a job? All that stuff. It starts to worry me too, after a while. If something is said enough times, you can really start to believe there's a problem. Personally, I'm sure I could manage all of these things if I wanted to. Sometimes my parents have been a little over-encouraging about academia, not netball or dancing or anything that involves flinging your limbs around. Naturally, that would be a coincidence, wouldn't it? They're not parents from hell. So to redeem them, I will say that they have now given up interfering. It became clear that when they were giving me all their advice, I was unlikely to be listening. It's a good trick.

Actually, my parents are a fascinating pair. They are from two completely different parts of India, with separate and unrelated cultures and languages. They both came to live in London in the sixties and that's where they met and married (unarranged). They are both very broad-minded, particularly my mother. She comes from a more liberal background than my father and I think she had a wild time in this country in the sixties. She travelled all over the world to places like Russia and Poland. She is pretty extraordinary. Sometimes, I get embarrassed if we're watching something really outrageous on TV, but then she just reminds me that she was here in the sixties – if she hasn't seen it already, it probably doesn't exist. I like to think that I've inherited some of that, but my attitude can be shocking sometimes and it annoys people. For example, I reckon it's quite profitable to be disabled – free travel, jobs that are open only to us and so on.

I'm quite clear on this; I wouldn't be made non-disabled, it's just not worth it.

The one thing about my identity that I am sure of is that I don't like being labelled 'Black'. People instantly think of African-Caribbean people first and then Asian people as a secondary thought. 'Black' gives strong representation to the primary group under that label, and to their long and strong history with which I cannot identify. Even if being lumped together like that means that both groups can occasionally help each other to create a more powerful image, I don't think its a good enough reason to pretend we have had the same experiences or want the same things. Black African-Caribbean people have a very different identity to Asian people.

So, my identity is important to me. I just haven't identified it yet. I hope there's no rush, because I don't think I'm going to manage it in the near future – the next forty years or so.

I'm sure my parents wish I was more solemn. I'm not a *supercrip*. I'm not *super* nice or *super* intelligent and I've never been particularly brave (yuk!) about being a disabled person. Actually, I'm a first-class wimp. I think, I might be a little bit normal.

Sita Ramprakash

In a Bengali Family

I have lived most of my life in Bangladesh, a small country in South Asia. My first glimpse of England was when I was ten. We flew in to Heathrow airport and stepped out on to a typical English day. The sky was covered with clouds which looked as if they were there to stay. The constant drizzle made me think that the weather suited my mood exactly.

How different this was from where I came from. The luscious greens I had known and loved for so long were no more, and in their place was the grey bleakness of the M4 motorway.

I had been too sheltered in those days to know about the many problems in my country; all I knew was the beautiful houses and the tons of relatives I had. I only knew the joys that Bangladesh offered and had no idea of the hardships, such as poverty and illiteracy. Most of my friends back in Bangladesh have remained sheltered in their upbringing and don't seem compelled to do anything about the state of our country. They are too busy with their studies and social life to have time, even if they did want to do anything. Many of my peers here are very concerned about the basic issues of poverty, illiteracy and inequality and how they still remain unresolved in our country. Perhaps if I still lived there, I would still be ignorant too.

There is a great difference between the rich and the poor in Bangladesh. Many wealthy people don't know or don't want to know the depth of poverty there. I think it makes them feel guilty about not trying to improve the situation.

I have no complaints about Bangladesh; all my memories from there are happy ones. The main reason behind this is my wonderful family. They have helped me through all my troubles and loved me for myself, or rather, in spite of myself. I can vividly remember the time when I failed my maths exam; I was so ashamed that I cried all the way home. It was my family who gave me confidence in myself when all I wanted to do was crawl under a rock and hide. They tutored me in turn so that by the time of the next exam, I had improved immensely. They have always been there for me and helped me through my problems no matter how big or small.

My greatest sorrow when I left Bangladesh, therefore, was leaving my family behind; my grandparents, uncles, aunts and cousins. Only my parents, my sister and I migrated, the rest of the family stayed behind.

Family life is the greatest source of joy and comfort

in Bangladesh, as elsewhere in Asia. Children are pampered and cuddled. Life revolves around the needs of the children in the family. Parents make plans for their children's holidays, careers and even marriage. This does not mean that children have no say in their own future. My parents have always taken our opinion into account before making decisions affecting us. All parents want the best for their children and any plans made for me would always be for my benefit.

In return, children are expected to be respectful to their parents, to obey their orders without much argument and to look after them in their old age. Older people in Asia have a much more dignified life than in the West. People would never think of sending their parents to old people's homes. Grandparents have a lot of authority in the family and even a forty-year-old son will ask his father's permission before buying a new car or having a holiday trip abroad.

Of course, things are changing slowly. For example, it is quite common now to find young couples living away from their parents, because of the needs of their jobs or because they prefer to lead a life entirely of their own.

Important occasions, such as weddings or naming ceremonies, bring the whole extended family together. They are joyous occasions. The loving bond between children and their parents is seen everywhere. A mother on the pavement, begging with her child at her breast will stop and rest in the shadow of a tree to cuddle her baby and sing it a lullaby.

Women play a vital role in the family. As a wife and mother, she looks after the needs of the family and in return she receives respect and love. But there are some people, especially country folk, who still think that men are better than women. They are happy if a new-born infant is male, for he is going to be their security in their old age. A girl is a bad investment; parents have to feed, clothe and educate her, and at the end of it all they have to offer a dowry to get her a good husband. Therefore, although daughters are loved dearly, some families will always feel a certain regret when a girl is born.

Coming to England has changed my life. I hope it is for the better, as I have grown to love this life. I don't think I would have had as much opportunity of further education in Bangladesh as I do here. I love the independence and equal opportunities given to me here. Maybe I don't love it in the same way as my life in Bangladesh, but don't we tend to forget the bad parts of our past and remember only the happy times? For instance, when I think of our home in Bangladesh, my memories are of the fun and games of my childhood; I try not to recall the death of my grandparents.

I will forever be thankful to my parents for bringing me here and providing for me. I feel I am a much better educated person here than I would ever have been back home. I have a much greater understanding of the world, rather than the narrow-minded way of thinking acquired by some Bengali children. For example, I have heard my peers say some very cruel and harsh things about the problems facing Bangladesh. I cannot speak for all the uncaring children of Bangladesh but I will never forget what a girl from a reasonably wealthy family once said to me while discussing the number of deaths due to poverty. She said, 'I don't know why you are so concerned. At least it keeps the population down.' I don't think Bangladesh has a future if its citizens have thoughts similar to this girl. I am glad to say that not all Bengalis are heartless. A lot of people are trying to make improvements in our country, but unfortunately, not enough so far.

I think I am more tolerant towards other people and their beliefs, but there is no denying the fact that there is a sharp contrast between what I am taught in school and what I am taught at home. At school, I am taught to think for myself and speak up against something I don't believe in. At home, I am told to respect what my elders say and believe what they tell me. I am taught never to argue with an elder. At school I am told men and women are equal, whereas at home I am begged to understand that men and women are not equal, they are just different. That doesn't mean that one is more important than the other, they both need to be treated with respect.

It is well known that women in developing countries are neglected, ignored and repressed. In the West, although women are educated and work alongside men in all professions, the male dominance of women has not ended. The situation is worse in developing countries where only twelve per cent of women have equal opportunities. Women in developing countries are very different from women in the West, they face different problems as the developed and developing have different social and economic structures, especially after colonisation. The main problem for women in developing countries is poverty, as opposed to the need to 'discover oneself', a goal of Western feminists.

So there are problems in both British and Bengali societies. The nature of the problems is different, but they have the same origins. It would be stupid of me to choose between the many different teachings of British society and Bengali society, because they are both right in their own way.

Sometimes, I think I have the best of both worlds but sometimes I think I am not really a part of either. Maybe I am on the outside of both and I cannot be accepted by either unless I let go of the other. But I can never let go without losing part of myself in the process.

Poonam Alam

Lucky Me

I am a fifteen-year-old Christian who has lived in England for thirteen years. I spent the first two years of my life where I was born in Sri Lanka. I have a twenty-year-old sister and a fourteen-year-old brother, who were also born in Sri Lanka. It was also the place where my parents were born and where they grew up.

My parents mean everything to me. They are the most important people in my life. My mother is a General Practitioner and my father is a consultant pae-diatrician. They really inspire me because they have both done so well – they both qualified in Sri Lanka and came to England with hardly anything. They have persevered and worked their way to the top. They have modified our house – we have several televisions, a computer, expensive bikes and all the luxuries that make us a middle-class family.

Even with all the efforts they have made to fit in (my father really could be an English gentleman), they still haven't got over the culture shock. After well over ten years of living in England, they think they know the ways of the land, but they grew up in Sri Lanka and that's where they were made into the wonderful people that they are. I don't think I will ever see a day when my parents will understand fully the concept of modern Britain. I could say that they're old-fashioned, but that would mean old-fashioned in English terms, when the truth is that a lot of Asian parents think like them.

I get asked a lot of questions by my parents when I go out, and I have to give fairly detailed descriptions of my plans, although my brother rarely gets asked more than two questions, and he's younger than me. My parents have a dim view of late nights and boyfriends, and expect a lot from all three of us. I don't have to work as hard as my parents had to in Sri Lanka, because they had to work extremely hard to get anywhere, as university places were limited and they didn't have much money.

My parents don't settle for anything less than full marks. I get a lot of pressure about school work, but so do my other Asian friends. Mum and Dad sometimes say that as long as I've done my best, it doesn't matter what my grades are, but I just know that they want me to be pulling in As by the odd comments and looks that I get when they look at my books or projects. I've learned to cope, but it's not easy. It would be easier to give in and settle for average grades, like any average British teenager, but knowing how disappointed my parents would be is enough to drive me to work harder. I am aware that failing is easier when the standard is so high. My delight at getting a B+ for a project is short-lived as it is followed by an in-depth analysis of my work and all the spelling mistakes are pointed out. A swift reminder of how clever my parents were when they were young also follows. After these anecdotes, I am left feeling not congratulated but cut down; this means that the next time I have an assignment, I try harder not to disappoint them.

Even with this pressure and hassle from my parents, I know that I'm extremely lucky to have them. Their 'emotional blackmail' forces me to do my work, and I prefer that to them not caring about my work at all. They look after me well and give me everything I want and need. It makes me realise how much they love me and care for my future. They only want the best for me.

But their culture shock also extends to my friends – they don't seem to understand why teenagers want to meet for the sake of having fun! Just because *they* like staying in, they consider that a good enough reason to force me to stay in too. They don't understand that rules that may have been relevant in Sri Lanka thirty years ago are just a bit ridiculous in London today. They assume that all the boys I know have one-track minds, but that's just a figment of their (prejudiced) imaginations. It's quite unfair of them to think like this, because while they trust my younger brother implicitly, they believe that all other boys are corrupt. They still don't understand the meaning of dating – they think the sexes shouldn't mix too much. We should only keep an eye on the opposite sex in case we see someone suitable for marriage. I know it sounds ridiculous, but this is the way it happened with them, their friends and all their relatives, and they seem to believe that English people do it this way too. According to my parents, the rule is not to go out with anyone until we are twenty-five, but, if we find someone suitable before then, we can marry at twenty-one! All three of us had to argue this out with our parents, but I think it will always be a topic that they will have difficulty getting their heads around.

I keep most of these feelings inside me. Perhaps in a few years, all these things that annoy me now will be unimportant. Perhaps, later on, I'll kick myself for getting so worked up and wasting energy on fighting about things. Sometimes I do have short bursts of anger and my parents seem to listen at the time, but then, when I've calmed down, everything goes back to the way it was before. When I do feel down, I keep my sanity by watching comedy programmes and funny films. My sense of humour keeps me going and I realise that, even if things are bad, I can at least laugh. Things could be worse; I could be homeless and not have a TV to watch, or my life could be such a mess that any amount of jokes couldn't make me laugh. It teaches me to look on the bright side of life, where so many great things are happening.

I am lucky to have lots of friends from different backgrounds around me. The friends that I spend most of my free time with are British or have extremely lenient parents. This means that a lot of these friends can't really identify with me, or understand the (sometimes ridiculous) demands made on me by my parents. My friends might also be pressured into working hard, but they also have a lot more freedom. I do find it aggravating that they can go out when I have to stay in and work, but then I justify it to myself by saying that otherwise, I would never have got the work done.

I have learned a lot from my parents, because they are realistic and haven't lost their heads. It would be easy to slip in some of British society's evil ways, but they have never lost their sense of morality. For example, the National Lottery is a tempting way to gamble away your money, help charities to lose income and encourage poorer families to throw away the little that they have on tickets. I think it is turning Britain into a greedy, money-oriented nation, and I am proud to say that not one member of my family has bought a ticket or ever will. I like to think that my parents have instilled these morals in me too and that they make me a better person.

Also, if it wasn't for my parents and my Asian roots, I probably wouldn't be lucky enough to have my religion. I am Christian. Some people have said that I am turning on my Asian roots, but it is, after all, the same God we all worship, so I've never had a problem with it. I think people without religion in their lives really miss out.

I'm lucky – I am grateful to be Asian and I have a loving family that have shown me the wonders of Christianity (something that even a lot of English people have missed out on). My Sri Lankan origin means that I have contact with a large family. I can travel almost anywhere in the world and find a relative to stay with! A large family also means that if I need help with school work, I have a lot of aunts, uncles and cousins to choose from. They are also good when it comes to choosing careers – because they are such a diverse group, I find that I am related to people who are in jobs that I might consider.

With my parents, faith and large family, I know that I will never have to be alone. I think I have the best of all worlds. I have no identity crisis, because even though I'm British, I'm really happy being Sri Lankan too. I don't feel less British for eating rice and curry with my fingers, and I don't feel less Sri Lankan for being Christian. Being an Asian woman in my shoes is great and I wouldn't trade places with anyone.

Gitanjali Vijeratnam

Singing Star

My name is Annapurna, which means goddess of food. I am fourteen years old, five foot, six inches tall and I have black hair and big black eyes. I'm quite shy (but not when I'm performing).

I was born in England and unfortunately I suffered some brain damage at birth which affects the movement of my right thumb and fingers. When I was young, I thought everybody had a hand like mine when they were little.

I come from a very musical family. My father was an Ustaad (master) in music. He was a highly talented and famous musician and he toured around the world. Unfortunately, he had a stroke in 1989 when I was eight and passed away. I never cried. I asked my mum to buy me a new dad from the shops. I miss my dad very much, but I am grateful and proud of my mum who brought me up in such a beautiful way. She is also a talented professional singer and music teacher, who has taught and guided me in my career as well.

I have been very musical, almost since I was born. My mum says that when I was two, I was at nursery singing and holding a stone as if it was a microphone! From then, Mum taught me Indian music scales on a keyboard, and I would learn more things by watching my mum and dad. When I was about six, I composed a song to Lord Krishna. It was an eight-beat afternoon raga and Mum and Dad were very proud of my composition. By the age of seven, I was playing the tambourine at performances my parents gave.

I also started acting courses, some in English and others in Hindi. At junior school, I sang in concerts and was very popular and happy. My best friend was Gurjinder, who couldn't speak English. I felt sorry for her because the other children ignored her, so I supported her because I spoke Hindi. In turn, she was very helpful and caring, especially when I couldn't use my hand.

When I started secondary school, it was a bit difficult. At first I enjoyed it, but it was hard to adjust as all the other pupils were white and I didn't know anybody. I went to that school because of my special needs and I tried hard to fit in. When I won the title 'Best Singer in 1994' my mum told the headteacher, who announced it to the class. This upset some of the white girls, who bullied me really badly. They did things like block my way when I wanted to get through a door and hid things like my pencil case.

I had no friends to sit with at lunch, so I went to

the welfare room to do my physiotherapy exercise for my hand. But the teachers said I had to go and sit with the other children. I was really terrified and I began to get scared of all white people. I didn't want my mum to know about this, in case talking about it made it worse. I used to cry secretly in my room and I began to hate going to school. Then I started to get very bad headaches, which puzzled my mum. We went to doctors and opticians, but in vain; nothing worked. In the end, Mum found out from my school report that some girls were dominating me. When she asked me about it, I burst into tears and finally told her everything.

Mum was very upset and complained to the head-teacher and the education officer, and I changed school to the one I am in now. I am very excited to be here, because I am going to school with more Asian girls, but I am still scared of bullies.

A few months later, I started to get a burning sensation in my head, which affected my whole body. I couldn't feed myself, write or concentrate. I ended up missing school for six weeks. I tried everything – going to hospitals, and praying. I even had to see a psychiatrist, but he couldn't work out what it was. People began to say that it was all in my mind. I felt so horrible. Then one day, my mum checked up on one of my blood tests and found that it was not right. She forced the doctors to put me on antibiotics. A week later, I felt much better. The psychiatrist thought that my mum had worked magic!

Slowly, with Mum talking to me and helping me to

build up my confidence, I gradually got better. I started performing in small concerts and luckily, a reporter from the local paper came to see one of them. The reporter wrote an article about how thrilling it was to see me dance and hear my voice and said I was like Whitney Houston! They took a colour picture of me and it was on the front page! Then I got on to Star Search on Asianet TV. My mum and family were so proud of me and many people praised me. Now I have fans all over and I am very confident on stage. I can smile and act and express my emotions in my work. I choreograph my own dances, which are sometimes hard to do, because of my disability. When I perform, it makes me feel very wanted and happy. I get lots of love and affection from my audiences, people from all races. I value them very much. I especially love older people, who touch my cheeks with their soft hands and bless me when I have sung religious songs to them.

So, my experiences with white people have been very mixed. Even though they do not understand the language exactly, they appreciate my dancing and singing. So far, they seem to respect me and my work when they are in the audience.

At my present school I love Art, French, History and English, but I am a bit slow at Maths. I love playing football and netball, outdoor PE and swimming, but there are some limits to what I can do. For example, I can't dive into the pool and sometimes I get frustrated when I watch other people do it.

My ambition is to become a singing star and I want my voice to travel the world. I want to work hard and sing in as many languages as possible, winning people's hearts. I would like people to see my talent and love me for it, and in turn, I will love them through my songs.

Annapurna Mishra

Rules and Regulations

I am Scottish with an Indian heritage. I was born in the UK, but my parents were born in India. They met in medical college and came to Britain for their training over 25 years ago. They always mention going back to India.

My parents don't seem to see my point of view; they don't understand what I want. They have lots of rules and regulations for me. They restrict me by not allowing me out after dark. I've just moved out of home and now they *phone* me all the time – they call me at 6 pm to make sure that I'm in from college and staying there until the next morning! All my friends have passed that stage. If they trusted me more, I wouldn't abuse it. I don't go out much anyway – only about four times in the last six months. It is my choice – I could have gone more often, but I didn't want to continually go behind their backs. That's probably the worst thing I've done – gone out when they have told me not to – but I feel so guilty when I get found out. Sometimes, it's not even just for me. For example, I've got one friend who has a boyfriend, so she asks me to go out with them, to keep the boyfriend's friend company. I've got nothing in common with him and I feel dead uncomfortable. So I'm just doing her a favour, being a good friend, getting nothing out of it and I'm the one who gets found out and told off. I can't even tell my mum that I'm only doing a friend a favour, because she'd freak – boy aren't allowed near me either!

I've got one really close male friend, he calls me his 'sister'. I went to visit him recently and Mum came with me for the whole time; she only left us alone for two hours, and even after that, when we came home, she asked me what I had done with him. We're just dead good friends, but my mum doesn't see it like that. My mum always wants to know *everything* about me, all the time. One step out of line and she ends up trusting me even less! My parents always tell me that they worry about me – I know they do, they don't have to keep telling me. Certain incidents don't help either, like, one of my male friends got drunk and phoned me at home at three o'clock in the morning! Mum and Dad totally freaked and asked why I had given out my number. In fact, they found out who the boy was and told his parents – it was so embarrassing!

So they're a bit strict. My white friends generally have less strict parents, but I have got one Asian friend who has only just turned seventeen, and her parents give her money, even though they know that she's going out and getting pissed at an over 18's club with it! I can't grasp the concept of having parents like that! I can't even reason with mine – like my dad – if he says something, he'll stick to it, even when he's wrong. Sometimes, my mum can be on my side and sticks up for me, but other times, she'll actually tell my dad on me! I'm more scared of my dad than I am of my mum.

Even my friends are intimidated by my parents. When I question my parents about it, they act all innocent. They would definitely say if they met a friend who they didn't like!

I have to keep secrets from my parents all the time, especially about my sister. My sister is four years older than me and she is a lesbian. If I've got a problem, I know I can count on her and she'll always be there for me. She is studying away from home at the moment. We get on much better since she moved away and we talk to each other quite a lot. No matter how long my parents have been in this country, I don't think they will ever be broad-minded enough to accept her if she came out to them. When she came out to me, I wasn't bothered at all. But now I feel bad because of the homophobic people at college. I'm always arguing with them. When I know somebody's wrong I will argue with them. Also, even in psychology class, the teacher went around asking all the girls if they had *boyfriends* and I thought that she should really have been asking if anyone had a *partner*!

I haven't confided in anyone else about my sister, because she asked me not to. I was about eleven or twelve years old when she told me – I'm not even sure

111

if I knew exactly what it meant. I remember she got a lot of hassle at school. It's quite funny really, my mum keeps asking me questions about my sister, like 'Has she got a boyfriend?' I always say that I don't know, but I think she knows I'm lying. I would like to be closer to my mum, she's always trying to be friendly and get me to talk to her more, but then she starts asking me too many things and getting nosey.

My parents are also trying to influence my career. They want me to be something like a lawyer, but I can't see myself as a lawyer. I've applied for physics and optometry – optometry is more of a career, so they prefer it. But, if I could choose to do anything, I would do photography as a degree. I've put it as one of my choices, and also architecture, which I am really into, but my parents aren't convinced.

I have got an unconditional offer from a local university to do physics, and Mum and Dad want me to take it. But I don't want to stay near my parents. They think everywhere else is dangerous. But I'm not going to give up. I want to go to Manchester – it's my first choice. My parents keep comparing me to others as well – one Bengali boy my family knows did what his parents wanted him to do; they chose his career, college, exam subjects, everything, so now they keep asking why I won't do the same and do as they tell me.

Some of my friends have asked me to try things that I'm not allowed by my parents – I have had alcohol – but I didn't feel pressurised at the time. But I think I would give in if they did pressurise me, because I think I'm easily led. There is no pressure about things like drugs, because they've already tried it and passed that stage already! I have been a bit tempted, but I haven't tried any myself; I've probably had some passive fumes though!

There is racism at home. We live outside a city and there are no other Asians in our neighbourhood. My parents find this difficult. We have names called at us and our windows smashed. Because my dad's the local doctor, they think we have a lot of money – big house in the country sort of thing – and they say 'You're not from this country, go back'. When we reported it to the police, they just waited to see if it would happen again. The police have said that having money is more likely to be the reason for the attacks, not racism. I don't get called things in the street near home, that only really happens in town, so I don't go to town very often. When I do go, I'll go in a group of friends. I don't feel threatened, but I won't walk home on my own if I can help it – my mum might come and meet me. I do tend to keep quiet when incidents happen, but I get mad inside.

When I get angry, I'm not sure where I put it. I think I do take it out on people, like maybe my parents when I answer back to them. I know I shouldn't, but I do. I don't tell them when racist things happen, I just tell my friends. But it's hard, because I personally think I am Scottish: my parents came here to make a better living. I'm perfectly equal with everybody. I don't think it matters where you come from.

I've got very religious parents who worship every Sunday. They try to make me go but I don't believe in it much and I don't want to contradict my own opinions. My parents keep trying to get me involved – it's like emotional blackmail. We do puja and celebrate Diwali, but not much happens in our area or in the nearest city. My generation don't really understand doing puja – it's all in Bengali. I understand it a bit, but it's all really ancient language. We know he's saying a prayer, but don't know what it means. Diwali is good; I really like it because it brings in all the culture, like dancing and I enjoy that. Most of my college friends are Pakistani Muslim and I tried fasting with them once, because I felt guilty eating in front of them. I'm not that bothered about religion – I don't know if that's wrong or right – I mean, who knows whether religion is right? We did more for Christmas really, but now that I have left school, I don't really do that anymore either.

At the moment, I don't do much from my culture and I only know what my parents tell me. I do sometimes cook Indian food at home – my mum helps me. As for traditional clothes, I would like to wear them. All my other friends have got shalwar kameez, and I think wow, I want one, but I don't want to ask my mum to get one because she doesn't have the same taste as me! Some of her saris are nice and I wear them for special occasions, like weddings and puja or Diwali. Mum and Dad speak in Bengali to me and each other, but I speak back in English. I have tried to speak Bengali, but I feel really stupid, because I know I can't pronounce it properly. I need more practice. Most of my friends took Bengali classes when they were younger, but I think I was influenced by my sister – because she didn't, neither did I!

The effect of keeping secrets from my parents and going against their rules is that sometimes I feel I have no one to turn to. I feel people are too busy to care, so I keep quiet about my troubles. I know that they do care; it's just that they've got other things on their plate. That's one of the bad things I do – bottle things up – then the problems get worse and don't get dealt with. It is at times like this that I get depressed and there's nothing anybody else can do to solve the problem. I also tend to think a lot by myself, I worry about things – parents, my future, everything. If I had a message for other Asian women, it would be to take things slowly, take your time, you'll get there eventually. Be sure of what you want – I still don't know – because then you can aim for it.

Tia

Keeping Up Appearances

It's late, a dark, dismal evening and the phone rings suddenly. My parents wake up, startled, in front of the TV. I shout that I will get it, as I have been expecting this call all evening. I run down, but my mum beats me to it, as if to say that whoever is on the other end of the line has to get through her first. (I always wondered how, despite complaining that aromatherapy didn't work on her bad back, she could amazingly sprint to the telephone and reach it before me every time.) She calls out my name, as if I'm not already on my way and I take the call. Mum is now pretending to continue watching TV whilst concentrating on what I am saying. I finally run to the bathroom and take the call there.

I'm met with Yaz's hysterical laughter on the other end of the phone; Mum has called me 'Shahreen', emphasis on the second 'h', the way it should be pronounced. Dad chose it from the Quran, but nobody says it like that except my parents. Everyone else pronounces it 'Shareen'. You're probably wondering what the big deal is over my name? Well, it seems to sum up my life. To my parents I'm Shahreen, the dutiful, obedient and 'oh-so-wide-eyed-and-innocent' daughter. At home, you won't catch me in low-cut body tops or tight hipsters, smoking a spliff, stoned out of my brain. Yet once I leave that front door, a sudden metamorphosis occurs. (Well, a bit premeditated actually.) Off comes the strait jacket and out comes 'Shareen' – a natural Gemini, creative, flirtatious, impetuous, hip chick. Some may say this is two-faced. I don't think this is the right word. Dual personality is more like it. Juggling two roles in one life, never a dull moment.

I have a pretty cool family, really. I know it would be more galvanising if I had a broken home, schizophrenic siblings, sexual or psychological abuse and so on. But no such tragedy has prevailed, and Inshallah (God willing), it won't. However, I wouldn't say that it has been an easy ride growing up Asian in Britain. As an Asian woman, I still have to reflect the morals and ideals of my family and community, especially of my father. My father is revered and respected as a figurehead, the 'maulavi'. He teaches the Quran to children all over West London, in mosques or at home. So the whole West London Bengali community thinks they know all about me and who I am through him.

The worth of an Asian girl is defined by how she conducts herself and who her family is – where the grains of her existence descend from. So as far as the community is concerned, I'm the maulavi's daughter, bas. Therefore, I must behave in a particular way or should be a particular person. A girl as an individual is rare, if not non-existent. I believe that the Asian community likes to mould girls into a certain type or stereotype. This moulding suffocates individuality and prevents social change, which is necessary if our generation is to survive in a country where, despite being born in it, you are reminded of your alien identity constantly.

I don't believe in disgracing your family and rocking the status quo in order to assert your individuality. You probably think I'm a hypocrite when I leave the house all 'goody-two-shoes' but when you meet me in a club, you won't recognise me from the next raunchy raver. Well, I don't care. You probably think I have a nerve, bragging about my lifestyle while my dad preaches religious dogma to unwitting children. I don't think that you should judge a person by how they appear, a mistake that our community makes all the time, which I think makes us bigoted and ignorant. For example, driving around an Asian area like Wembley, my mum will notice, like a hawk, a group of teenage girls gossiping and chattering away in a restaurant. She will point out how they are attracting unwanted male attention by sitting in public. Or my brother, on seeing a girl wearing anything which doesn't cover her from scalp to toe, will comment on why she isn't at home helping with the cooking. This attitude exasperates me no end and indicates how ignorant even your own family can be. The irony is that the girls they criticise could easily be me.

Many families feel that we are in danger of being unscrupulously corrupted by Western society. But my family are not that blind or gullible; they know that my best friend ran away from home, is a compulsive boozer and is currently shacked up with a dealer. But my friend is not me, and I appreciate that my family allowed me the benefit of the doubt when I told them that they need not worry about me becoming like her. Of course, I had the usual 'what will people say if they see you hanging around with her?', 'what about your father's "izzat" (honour) when they think you are just like her?' And, however much I loved her as my friend, I did not want to be the target for gossip or stick my neck out at the expense of my family's izzat. By seeing how her family were treated as lepers when everyone found out about her, I learned that there is a limit to how far you can go between the lines of decency and immorality – which are very thin. Asian girls have to shoulder this responsibility, however unfair it may seem.

But what about all the other Asian women, who are more passive and silent than me? I admire girls who wear shalwar kameez to school, who resist falling for a guy and experimenting with drugs. I can resist anything too, except temptation! I don't wear hijab, and will only wear shalwar kameez for a wedding – why? It's just not me. If I had been surrounded by girls wearing hijab, covering themselves from head to toe, if I had gone to a girl's school, if all my friends had been doing the same, then maybe I would have turned out differently. I do find it hard to satisfy the two personas that I have, Asian Muslim girl versus British teenager.

Sometimes I do feel trapped and conscience-stricken that I can't be open about the other side of me. I know it would break my parents' hearts and cause scandal if I was more open, but I don't think I've done anything wrong. I don't feel guilty about having secret relationships, or that at the back of my wardrobe I keep very sexy PVC outfits that I wouldn't dare show my mother. I don't think I'm deceiving my parents – snigger if you must. They know I'm opinionated, that I voice my thoughts about everything from pop to politics. I think that, secretly, they are proud that I can think for myself, but, like all Bengali parents, they fear that too much knowledge will make me rebel. (I say Bengali parents specifically, because I know other Indian parents who are supportive of their daughter's education). That's why most Bengali girls will finish A levels and then sit at home refining their fish-cleaning skills whilst waiting for a marriage proposal. My parents have learned not to expect that from me. I've allowed them to run parts of my life simply because they are my parents, not because I trust them as individuals. The Quran says that 'paradise lies at the feet of one's parents' and I love mine as all children love their parents. But there are some things that I don't want to have dictated to me by my parents or Allah.

Many non-Asian people get a very blurred image of what Asian girls are like when they meet me. My current boyfriend is French–Canadian. He didn't ask me out for weeks because one of my friends joked that I was engaged to a boy in Bangladesh and he believed her! I've never been out with an Asian guy. I would like to, but there's too much of a risk of gossip in the community. Most of the guys I've dated are fascinated by my life – they think it's hilarious when I suddenly have to let go of their hand when walking down the street and rush ahead, on spotting someone I know. The 'people talk' factor is high in every Asian girl's life and Bengalis must be masters of this art, knowing that with every word, a reputation dies. I think that I have managed to steer clear of the gossips' vicious tongues, but then again, you can't be too sure. I think most of the 'bad reputations' are unfounded, but it's one of the first things that a family will look for when searching for a bride. Even a slight blemish can do untold damage. Maybe my turn is inevitable? I'm not ashamed to say what I'm not ashamed to think, and I don't want to turn into a recluse to avoid being talked about.

My current guy is beginning to get frustrated; he's slept with all his other girlfriends and I am adamant about preserving my virginity for my husband. I do know many Asian girls who aren't virgins, and it's their prerogative. At least most of them have lost 'it' to long-term partners. My white and Black friends still think that monogamy is a type of wood! They bed hop like a bunch of demented Duracell bunnies! It doesn't impress me. Asian guys are the same, just interested in the thing between their legs. What infuriates me is the blatant double standard that they have – one rule for their girlfriends and another for their sisters. When are all these 'protective' men going to realise that the girls

121

that they ogle at are someone else's sister? My four brothers have made no bones about the fact that if they ever caught me doing anything untoward, they would make me regret it! Every Asian guy I've liked is friends with at least one of my brothers – some things aren't worth losing a limb for! I suppose that part of that is them looking out for me, but part is male ego – it's macho to be protective and uphold family honour – and they end up being tyrants. I remember one occasion when a cousin's friend was driving around yelling at girls. He alternately called them slags for not wearing hijab or asked them to come with him. To his dismay, one of his 'babes' turned out to be a relative! The noble machismo act goes out of the window when they want to satisfy their male virility. It just shows that Asians tend to adopt morality as an attitude towards those they personally dislike. My message is, if the men aren't going to be celibate, don't expect the girls to behave like nuns!

However, the Bengali culture is a strong influence on my life, even though it doesn't produce Bollywood-style films; and doesn't have a long, mythical history like India; or national heroes, like Imran Khan for Pakistan. The community spirit and kinship upon which Bengali's thrive is something to be proud of.

My relationship with Allah is that of obedience and service – it's very personal. I pray five times a day because I believe in it; I want to acknowledge God's mercy every day. I admit that when I was younger, I did everything to get out of praying. I hated getting my ears wet when we had to do 'wazu'. Now I pray

122

and read the Quran without coaxing. I'm not trying to sell myself as a good Muslim to anyone; I don't need to prove anything because at the end of the day, God decides my fate, not mere mortals. Of course, I could do more to be a better Muslim, but everyone takes advantage of God once in a while. I remember reciting one sura (verse of the Quran) before a maths exam. I'm not sure what I expected – some sort of divine intervention to remember Pythagoras's Theorem? No, it just makes me feel like someone is listening to me and if something makes me content, I remember that it is all down to Him. I believe that culture and religion needn't be a hindrance for Asian women. If we can be proud of our heritage on festival days such as Eid, why can't we retain that pride for the rest of the time?

At times I wonder whether it will be my generation of young women who will grow up to be the ones that initiate a new type of family life and help our societies to accept the cliché that 'times are changing'. I hope it is. Progress is impossible without change and change is necessary to prevent us from living a lie.

Shahreen Khan

Contributors' Notes

Leila is a nineteen-year-old practising Pakistani Sunni Muslim. She is the youngest of four sisters and one brother. She is currently applying for media courses and she is working on a novel. Her hobbies include writing Urdu poetry, and listening to classical Indian songs. She loves English autumns and hates religious fanatics and macho men. She continues to be in hiding from her family.

Mina is sixteen years old and of Indian Sunni Muslim heritage. She has one older and one younger sister. Her oldest sister has just had an arranged marriage. Mina's favourite subject at school is English and her ambition is to be a journalist. There isn't much to do in her village, but she enjoys listening to the radio. She really hates not having her own space, as her family likes being involved in everybody else's business, including hers!

Tia recently turned eighteen. She is Scottish-born, but of Bengali heritage. She lives in a rural area about an hour's drive from a large Scottish city. She would love to visit India in order to explore her roots, and travel to other places, like America. She loves being with her friends; and she hates having to compromise, which she feels she has to do, rather than stick to what she wants.

Jill Akera is of Punjabi Indian origin, and her family is Sikh, but not practising. She is an only child and lives at home with her parents. Her GCSEs are over, and she's not sure what to do next. She wants to work in the clothing industry, preferably in fashion design. Her hobbies include going out with friends and listening to English and bhangra music. She dislikes being asked the same question over and over again!

Halema Begum Aktar is sixteen and of Bengali heritage. Her family is Sunni Muslim, but not very strictly practising. Her family consists of three brothers and five sisters. Her favourite subjects are business, art and history, and she will be studying business at college. Her ambition is to be a nurse. Her main hobby is reading and she also enjoys gardening with one of her sisters and phoning friends for a chat. What irritates her most is her youngest sister, who really knows how to get on her nerves!

Poonam Alam was born in Bangladesh and lived there until she was ten years old. Quite a strict practising Muslim, she lives at home with her parents, younger sister and grandmother. She is currently preparing for her GCSEs next year. Her favourite subjects are science and geography, but she aims to do maths and information technology A levels in order to lead to an accountancy degree. She enjoys reading, creative writing and watching TV and her ambition is to make her parents proud of her.

Farah Aly is nineteen and a Shia Muslim. She is currently living away from home at university, but she would normally live with her parents and younger brother. She is of East African Indian heritage but was mainly brought up in Britain. She is keen to get her degree, but is not quite sure what she will do with it when she graduates. Her hobbies include creative writing and art and she likes to think of herself as 'environmentally friendly'. She loves the smell of freshly cut grass and hates queuing for the bathroom!

Shabneet Chadha is sixteen and lives in an extended family of parents and two younger sisters, plus her father's youngest brother, his wife and two children. Her family originates from a village in Pakistan called Thalwandi, and they left during the partition of India and Pakistan. Her favourite subjects are English, drama and science and she hopes to pursue a career involving medicine. She enjoys reading, going out and eating and would love to play a lead role in a play. The best thing in the world is Chinese food and she really hates male chauvinist pigs!

Valene Coutinho is nearly sixteen years old, a practising Catholic, with a fourteen-year-old younger brother. Her first name originates from the character in Dallas, which was popular when she was born, and her surname is Goan Portuguese, as her father is from there. Her mother is half-Italian and half-Madrasi and so Valene identifies herself as Indian. She loves art and English at school and intensely hates science and maths! She would like to aim for a career in the Arts, such as graphic design or fashion design. She likes music by TLC, Madonna, Mariah Carey and Alanis Morissette. Watching the movie *Dirty Dancing* will always cheer her up, but one thing that really infuriates her is her brother putting on Teletext when she's watching something on TV!

Salima Dhalla is seventeen and a Shia Muslim. She lives with her parents and her younger sister, and she wants to be a doctor. She loves travelling, keep-fit and then eating to make up for keeping fit, and watching action films.

Harsha Dhokia is a Hindu of East African Indian heritage. Her favourite subjects at school include art and design. She would love to have a career in design, but is doing more research into it before she makes a final decision. She loves being creative with her hands and enjoys cooking Indian curries. She would like people to like and respect her for who she is, rather than for what she looks like or what she's wearing.

Raj Kelair is sixteen and of Punjabi origin. Her family is Sikh, but not practising. She has just finished GCSEs and will be going to college to study media, psychology and English literature for A level. She lives with her parents and two younger sisters, and her hobbies include reading, playing piano, skiing and writing. She likes to take part in charity events including the Strollerthon, a ten-mile walk around London, and 24-hour fasts. She loves a good argument and hates being bored!

Shahreen Khan is currently applying for university, having made the choice to become a lawyer. She is a Muslim of Bengali heritage and is the youngest in her family. She has four older brothers and one older sister. They were all born in Bangladesh, except her youngest brother. She used to enjoy being the youngest, but now it's more like having lots of parents, so sometimes she'd prefer to be an only child! She loves chatting on the phone to friends and socialising, and hates ignorance in people. Whenever she's feeling down, she listens to the song 'Stand By Me' by Ben E King and it always cheers her up.

Nina Miah is nineteen and currently in her second year at university, studying law. She was born in Bangladesh, the oldest of seven sisters and one brother. She lives at home with them, her parents and two grandmothers. She hopes one day to be a successful solicitor. Her hobbies are drawing and reading, especially Raymond Chandler crime novels, but at the moment it's mostly law books! What irritates her the most is when she's dressed up to go out and her younger sister says, 'You're not going out in that are you?!' Her best times are with her sisters and brother, when they are all at home and getting on well with each other.

Annapurna Mishra is fourteen and an only child. Her mother is from Mauritius and her late father was from Benares, but Anna was born in Britain. She would like to focus on a singing career and her ambition is to be a successful singer. She's happiest when she gets good grades for homework and hates to have an untidy house.

Shaheena Begum Mossabir is currently in her second year at university, where she has sacrificed her first love, English literature, in order to study law to ultimately help the people of her Bengali community with their rights. She is the third of six sisters and has two younger brothers, which means the women in her family get the upper hand! She enjoys reading and going out with friends and family, but nothing beats drinking tea and watching a good video with her mum.

Kalpna Patel is twenty-two and has lived in England all her life. She has completed a degree at Goldsmiths College and lives in London with a group of friends. She is currently working for London Weekend Television and hopes that one day she will become a producer for a successful television programme.

Rahila Punjwani is seventeen and of East African Indian origin. She is currently doing her A levels and her aim is to be an aid doctor. She loves travel and pizza and dislikes pop music.

Sita Ramprakash is twenty and an only child, who now lives in her own flat. Her mother is Sindhi and her father is Bengali and she was born in Britain. She has been a disability rights advocate for the past two years and is currently a line-dancing enthusiast. She loves food and hates exploitative government advertising campaigns which just use disabled people, for example, portraying them as a consequence of drink driving accidents.

Ishman Tardho is sixteen and was born in Britain. Her parents were both born in East Africa and are Gujarati in origin. Her favourite subjects are history, psychology and English, and she would like to go to university, but she's not sure what she'll be studying there. Her hobbies include playing 'different' sports like basketball and trampolining. She loves socialising with her friends and can't stand two-faced people, who say one thing and go and do another.

Niksha Thakrar is fifteen years old and was born in Britain. Her parents were raised in Uganda. She lives with her parents and grandfather, and she has an older brother who's twenty and away at university. Niksha speaks fluent Gujarati and has a Gujarati GCSE. Her favourite subjects are business studies, history and sociology, which she hopes to continue to A level. She aims to get a degree in business studies and eventually to own her own business. She likes listening to music, going out and studying.

Gitanjali Vijeratnam is fifteen and lives with her parents and an older sister and younger brother. They are all Christian and were born in Sri Lanka. Her favourite subjects include English and history, but she also likes the sciences and is considering careers in law or medicine. (But don't believe her, as her plans change every five minutes!) She likes singing and playing and listening to music. She hates it when her parents make up rules just for the sake of it.

grab a livewire!
real life, real issues, real books, real bite

Rebellion, rows, love and sex . . . pushy boyfriends, fussy parents,
infuriating brothers and pests of sisters . . . body image, trust, fear
and hope . . . homelessness, bereavement, friends and foes . . .
raves and parties, teachers and bullies . . . identity, culture clash,
tension and fun . . . abuse, alcoholism, cults and survival . . . fat
thighs, hairy legs, hassle and angst . . . music, black issues, media
and politics . . . animal rights, environment, veggies and travel . . .
taking risks, standing up, shouting loud and breaking out . . .

. . . grab a Livewire!

For a free copy of our latest catalogue,
send a stamped addressed envelope to:

The Sales Department
Livewire Books
The Women's Press Ltd
34 Great Sutton Street
London EC1V 0DX
Tel: 0171 251 3007
Fax: 0171 608 1938